ABOUT THE AUTHOR

John Griffiths – original surname, Francis – was born, raised and educated in Swansea. After university and teacher training, he moved to London in 1970 and taught English and Drama in a couple of Ealing schools before becoming a professional actor in 1978.

Since then he has toured over a dozen African countries in Shakespeare productions for the British Council; played in Canada twice: in *Oliver!* and *The Boyfriend*; done five seasons in Sweden; performed all over Europe and the UK; worked extensively in rep, in film, on TV and radio; made several original cast recordings; spent two years as a National Theatre player; appeared in seven West End shows; played seasons at The Open Air Theatre, Regent's Park; Sadler's Wells; The Orange Tree and The Old Vic; taken two shows to the Edinburgh Fringe, including his adaptation of *The Gospel According to John*, a piece for solo performer. This production also toured cathedrals, churches and theatres as a Millennium project.

PREVIOUS WRITING EXPERIENCE

Two one-man shows: *Forty Years Gone; Chapel, Chums and Chips*; and a three-hander, *A Cock-and-Bull Story*.

David Harmer (Illustrator) lives in Surrey and is known locally as a watercolour artist. Drawing skills were learned during his working career, designing interiors for hotels and restaurants. Now retired, he paints a wide range of subjects: anything from cityscapes to animal studies. Elephants were favourites for a while; horses more recently; and now, of course, mice.

You can visit his website:
davidharmerwatercolour.co.uk

or follow his blog:
offtoafineart.com

THE WRITE ESCAPE

How one actor coped with Covid

JOHN GRIFFITHS

WITH ILLUSTRATIONS BY
DAVID HARMER

Matador
9 Priory Business Park,
Wistow Road, Kibworth Beauchamp,
Leicestershire. LE8 0RX
Tel: 0116 279 2299
Email: books@troubador.co.uk
Web: www.troubador.co.uk/matador
Twitter: @matadorbooks

ISBN 978 180046 382 0

British Library Cataloguing in Publication Data.
A catalogue record for this book is available from the British Library.

Printed and bound in Great Britain by 4edge Limited
Typeset in 10pt Adobe Garamond Pro by Troubador Publishing Ltd, Leicester, UK

Matador is an imprint of Troubador Publishing Ltd

This book is dedicated to two Swansea boys, both
Llewellyn,
who died within six weeks of each other in 2018:
Roger and Meic

SPECIAL THANKS ARE DUE TO

David for his charming mice.
Chris for her editing and proofreading.
Cec for her support and encouragement.
Andy for his technical wizardry.
Liviu for his portrait of the author.
Gaynor and Nick for their generosity.

CONTENTS

PREFACE

I have been used to changes in my life. That's not surprising for someone in his seventies. I was born and raised in Swansea in the immediate post-war period. After school, university and college, I took up a teaching post in an Ealing primary school in 1970. I loved teaching, even the tough year I spent as a team leader in a challenging school close to Wormwood Scrubs prison. Drama was my main subject and I was responsible for the annual Christmas productions. In my spare time I polished my acting skills at the celebrated Questors Theatre in West London – an amateur organisation with impressive facilities and high production values. But the pull of the stage was too strong and in 1977 I decided to try it professionally. This proved to be a wise move, which I have not regretted once. I have been very lucky. Until March 2020, that is, when all live performance was halted. For the second time in my life I experienced a career change, and decided to try my hand at writing. It seems like 'the write escape'.

ACKNOWLEDGEMENTS

John would like to thank:
Gareth Armstrong
Jane Dewey
David Evans at David Higham Associates
Liviu Enache Photography.
Barbara Fisher
Stephen & Hazel Francis
Nick & Gaynor Fraser
Leigh Fry
David & Margarette Harmer
Cecily Hughes
Roy Johnson at Troika Books
Andy Keelan
Kelly Jayne Meadows
David Roughan
Christine Secombe
Anthony & Beryl Singlehurst
Holly Wilson

(Not forgetting the extended *Facebook* family who encouraged this folly.)

INTRODUCTION

The Write Escape is an edited version of my daily blogs during lockdown, and covers the seven months from March to September 2020. But this is personal. I had been touring in *The Mousetrap*, Agatha Christie's record-breaking play.

This book shares my feelings on the triple loss of livelihood, colleagues and identity. It outlines the daily routine; charts the changing seasons; records good days and bad. Along the way we mark anniversaries, meet a host of interesting people and discover some delicious recipes. Although it covers serious issues at a critical moment for the world, the overall tone is one of hope, and faith in the human spirit to adapt and survive.

CHAPTER 1

"BEWARE THE IDES OF MARCH"

6.32pm, Monday 16th March
Waterside Theatre, Aylesbury. An almost dark auditorium.

"Not happy with that blackout, Garry. Anything you can do?"

I was putting the question to our lighting designer on the tour of Agatha Christie's *The Mousetrap*. It was part of my job as resident director to ensure that at the end of Act One the stage should be as dark as we could make it. Otherwise the play would cease to be a murder mystery: the cat truly would be let out of the bag.

As Garry sets about his task there's a tap on my shoulder: it's the Theatre Manager:

"Don't worry about it, John. There'll be no show tonight in this or any other theatre. We've just received a directive from above."

Terrible timing. Some playgoers are already pressing into the bar and foyer, ordering their drinks, buying programmes,

1

anticipating an enthralling evening ahead from the 'Queen of crime'.

The whole company gathers in the Green Room where the theatre has laid on drinks for us all. These would normally be drunk *after* the first night's performance not *before*; it doesn't feel right. The atmosphere is gloomy and tense. We drown in a flood of questions. *What is happening at this moment front of house? Are some of the people angry? Or are they just disappointed?* After all, they've probably been planning this for a while. A chance to see this iconic play at last. *Have they come far? Are some demanding refunds? Are others philosophical and patient? Will the theatre be insured, or will this be judged to be 'Force Majeure'?*

And what about the workers? If the rest of the run is cancelled, will we be paid? What is the contractual position? How will Equity, the actors' union, react? As actors invariably do in a crisis, we adjourn to the pub.

*

The White Hart is very busy for this time on a Monday. It looks more like last orders on a Saturday night. Perhaps the punters sense that when "Time" is called tonight it might last considerably longer than normal. We manage to find a table, almost colliding with a dodging waiter who is trying to control a shaky snake of pint glasses in the crook of his arm. Our questions continue to ebb and flow as we enjoy a glass or two. *What about the Irish leg? We're due in Dublin in a fortnight. They might have different rules. It's a foreign country after all. There are Scottish and Welsh dates on the schedule, too. What will those devolved administrations decide?*

I phone a friend – Annie Hamilton-Pike (or H.P. for short). It's only been four hours since she dropped me off at the Stage Door:

"Hello, love. Show's cancelled. Can you come and pick me up, please? I'm in The White Hart, opposite Waterside, next to the car park."

"Of course, darling. I'll be there in twenty minutes."

Originally the plan had been that H.P. and her friend Pete should have come to see the show that night, but they had both decided that in the circumstances it might be wise not to sit in a confined space with coughing strangers for over two hours. With the benefit of hindsight, they were right.

As well as being my chauffeur, H.P. was to have been my theatre landlady for the week. Her house in Hyde Heath only a short car ride from the venue.

What's going to happen?

I spend a restless night.

The next morning we hear from Tim, our Company Manager, that the play is cancelled for the whole week, and that we will be paid pro-rata only and not in full. Also that the show is suspended until further notice. We can return to the theatre anytime until 5.00pm to clear our stuff from the dressing rooms. Later, going into 'my' room, which it never really became, feels odd and unsettling. In fact, at the risk of being melodramatic, this must rank as one of the saddest moments in my forty-two thespian years. *Why am I packing up when not one word of the play has been spoken in this space, and its boards remain untrodden?* No, this is all wrong.

Whatever happened to, "The show must go on"? Signing out, I exchange a few choked words with the Stage-Door Keeper:

"Good luck." "And you." "Stay safe."

"You, too."

When we get back to Annie's, we decide that I will stop over for another night and that I will go home the next day. Wednesday morning, H.P. insists on driving me all the way back to Brentford as she doesn't want me to risk public transport. There's a dog in the car with us: Lola, a Jack Russell, fourteen. But there's an elephant, too: Covid-19. Small talk distracts us for a while, but inevitably we keep returning to the same subject: *the virus*, and what it might mean. We ask dozens of questions, but have no answers. As we pass through Chalfont St Giles, where my agent, Lisa, lives, I call out as if she can hear me: "Lisa, I'll ring you later!" Pointless, of course, but strangely comforting.

When we get to 'London Town', as H.P. calls my patch, she turns down the offered coffee, and after she and Lola have both had comfort breaks, one in the loo and the other up the alley, we say our spaced-out goodbyes; but not before we have promised to speak via WhatsApp every day for the foreseeable. She will ring on the odds and I will ring on the evens. A virtual, visual chat better than no contact at all.

For the first few days I get to know my flat again, as I have been on the road with Agatha for fifteen months, give or take a few brief holiday weeks. Friends and neighbours say my place is always pristine, but I know differently. It's only had a lick and a promise for months and is a stranger to a deep clean. So I set about it with a will. But first I make a list of what needs doing indoors and out:

Give the flat a good bottoming: shampoo the carpets; clean the brass and silver; polish the furniture; put winter clothes away in the loft and bring the summer gear down (*tempting fate?*); empty the fridge and freezer, defrost them, and then cook up a storm and fill them both. It's time to get a new fridge, too. A larder type, so an ice-box doesn't take up valuable storage space. After all, I can make ice in the freezer. While I'm indulging in retail therapy, I decide I need a new TV – the sound keeps going on the old one. I'll probably be watching more telly during lockdown. And I'm sure to be reading a lot so I really need a new lamp to light the area around the armchair. Not forgetting the dodgy doors on the kitchen cupboards. That's the problem, when you start looking for snags, they seem to multiply. There's certainly a lot to be done after a period of benign neglect. Which brings me to the garden. Roses want pruning; hydrangeas de-heading;

clematis cutting down to size. There's clearing and digging and feeding to be done. Pots to be emptied of exhausted soil, and after a thorough clean, freshly filled with compost. This is the ideal opportunity to grow my own vegetables, herbs and salads. But I'm not alone. Other people obviously have the same idea. Seeds are in short supply. I manage to buy two kinds of lettuce, tomatoes, rocket and basil. H.P. shares her carrots and beets with me. I read the instructions on the packets and start sowing the seeds indoors in pots and trays. When I run out of containers I improvise with empty cartons and tins that recently held yoghurt or baked beans. I sow, water and wait for the miracle of germination to begin.

By now it is the end of the first week. So far so busy. But I am beginning to wonder: *Should I still be going to the local supermarket?* It's very crowded, and the idea of social distancing is in its infancy; and it doesn't have many adherents in the Brentford branch of Morrisons. Many shelves are empty: pasta and toilet rolls are conspicuously absent. Perhaps, as I belong to an 'at risk' group, I ought to try to shop online. This proves to be problematic as the demand is high. There are many who are more deserving than me. Tommy and Pip, who live in the flat below mine, come to my aid; and for the next three weeks they do the supermarket shop for me. This is a godsend.

When I am beginning to think that this can't continue indefinitely, that I can impose on their kindness no longer, I manage to get a slot with Sainsbury's. A major problem solved. One has to eat to live. And I live to eat.

Being home of an evening is a novel experience. Round about 6.00pm, when I reach for a beer or a G&T, I can't help thinking what I would have been doing if Corona hadn't intervened and taken away my livelihood. I would have been arriving at the theatre around this time. More often than not a swift chat in the office with Tim, our company stage manager; a quick hello to Caroline in wardrobe; a check that all is well on stage; a gentle physical and vocal warm-up; catching up with fellow actors who are running through their usual pre-show preparations; and finally popping into the dressing rooms to wish everyone all the best for yet another performance:

"See you on the Green!"

"Toi! Toi!"

"Have a good one."

"Another full house."

Then, before you have time to say "Agatha Christie," the half is called by She-who-must-be-obeyed, our super-efficient deputy stage manager, Ela Schmidt. It's 6.55pm precisely:

"Ladies and Gentlemen of *The Mousetrap* company. This is your half-hour call. You have half an hour, ladies and gentlemen."

We have thirty minutes to get ready: time to check our props, set our water-bottles, get into costume and character – in my case the tweedy, cavalry-twilled, moleskinned, brogued, moustachioed old cove, Major Metcalf.

7.25pm: "Ladies and gentlemen of *The Mousetrap* company, this is your Act One beginners call. Act One beginners on stage, please."

7.30pm: Curtain up. Literally.

The Mousetrap was written at a time when the beginnings and ends of the acts were punctuated by the raising and the lowering of the front curtain. This tradition certainly serves this piece well, adding to the drama and suspense. At the top of *The Mousetrap*, the curtain rises on an empty stage. We are in the Great Hall of Monkswell Manor Guest House. It is dark apart from thin winter light spilling through an upstage window. Outside, falling snow can be seen. A magical opening.

I miss the routine, the play, the company and the audience more and more as the first lockdown week closes.

Saturday 21st March

Usually I would have been doing two shows, followed by packing up to go on to the next venue. Saturday was all go. Except now it's not. I can watch Saturday TV for the first time in months. It's been so long, I'd forgotten how disappointing the choices on the box are on that evening. Probably the worst programmes of the week. This paucity of quality

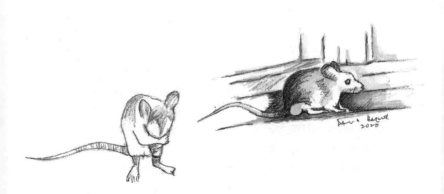

entertainment increases my nostalgia for live performance, and *The Mousetrap* in particular.

Throwing myself into all the domestic tasks is a distraction, of course, and helps fill my days. Then there's walking. I try to walk for an hour each day. And we are spoilt for choice in Brentford: docks, parks, a canal and two rivers – the Thames and the Brent – streets that offer a chance to go back to Georgian times. Evidence, too, of the English Civil War. The Battle of Brentford, 1642. Centuries earlier, Julius Caesar crossed the Thames in 54 BC. History is everywhere. And then we have Kew Gardens, a World Heritage site, a ten-minute walk away. That Saturday morning I use my membership card and go for a restorative stroll. I pass the allotments where a student is tending his plot, helped by his partner and their toddler. This act of faith, the knowledge that seeds sown now will still thrive despite the pandemic, is touching and uplifting. Nature is immutable.

What is *sown in sorrow*, will be *reaped in joy*.

Later in the Japanese garden a pause for breath... long and slow. Mindfulness among the rocks, plants and tumbling water. Just before leaving, I creep into my favourite and secret place: a circular seat under a pergola of wisteria, in bud but not yet in bloom.

This visit turns out to have been timely, as next morning, on opening my emails, I find one informing me that, acting on government advice, Kew Gardens will be closed until further notice. I shall have to be content with my own little plot, and St Paul's, the nearby recreation ground, for a while.

Sunday 22nd March

This is the first Sunday in many months that I haven't had to unpack, do laundry and sort out what I'm going to take with me for the next tour date. Sunday has not been a day of rest for a while. It's been a turn-around, catch-your-breath, see-some-friends-if-you're-lucky sort of day. But not this Sunday.

Time to pause and decide what I'm going to do to fill the creative gap in my life, now theatres are dark.

What I decide is this: every morning from now on, until lockdown ends and life reverts to normal, I shall start the day with three Ps. Nothing to do with a weak bladder. No, I will read a poem, a prayer and a psalm first thing with my early cuppa. There are 150 psalms, so restrictions are bound to be over by the time I reach the last one in five months' time. Who knows, perhaps the virus will have shot its bolt by then, and there will no longer be a pandemic?

Psalm 1 is a quiet meditation, full of hope. Ideal for this time of year: the end of winter and the budding promise of spring. But it seems to be more relevant than ever at this precise moment, a time of global crisis. The writer pledges:

"He shall be like a tree planted by the rivers of water, that bringeth forth his fruit in his season; his leaf also shall not wither; and whatsoever he doeth shall prosper."

A promising start.

I think this is also the ideal opportunity to dip daily into an anthology of poetry given to me a couple of years back by my friends Mac and Maggie Rogers: *A Poem for Every Day of the Year*.

The early offerings by Eleanor Farjeon and William Blake bristle with omens for warmer and brighter days ahead. I find myself in agreement with Christina Rossetti's claim that, "There is no time like the Spring." I sing/read the lyrics of 'A Morning Song', which most of us know as 'Morning has Broken', unable to get Cat Stevens' silky voice and the Gaelic tune out of my head; and I am suddenly back in assembly at Stanhope Junior School, where I took up my first teaching post in the seventies. Mr Bishop, the head teacher, hymn book in hand, is leading the singing at the front, while his deputy, Miss MacDonald, accompanies us at the piano. Four hundred voices unite in praise to God, celebrating His creation, which is new every morning. The teachers endure the unforgiving, bucket-backed, plywood chairs; the children sit cross-legged in uniformed rows on the shining herringbone floor.

Back to the present, and my third 'P': prayers. There is certainly no shortage of prayers to choose from each day. I opt for St Francis for starters. An obvious choice as my family name is Francis.

The most well-known lines of his, famously quoted by Mrs T on the steps of Number 10 in 1979, are not by him at all, but by an anonymous twentieth-century author:

Where there is hatred, let me bring love;
Where there is injury, pardon;
Where there is discord, union;
Where there is error, truth;
Where there is doubt, faith;
Where there is despair, hope;

Where there is darkness, light;
And where there is sadness, joy.

But these words, ancient or not, are perfect for this moment.

I love his authentic offerings, though, especially 'Brother Sun and Sister Moon': "Praised be you, my Lord, with all your creatures, especially our Brother Sun, Who is the day through whom you give us light…" St Francis finds God in the heavens and in the world around him, in the wind and weather, in all the elements, especially fire and water; but finishes on a practical note, coming back down to earth with a plea for "those who bear sickness and suffer trial." His words have a relevance and resonance for these dark pandemic days.

When 23rd March blows in I find it hard not to run through the well-practised Monday morning routine: early alarm, breakfast, pack and book an Uber to one of London's main railway termini: Paddington, Waterloo, Victoria, Euston, or St Pancras. This Monday it should have been King's Cross Station, and then the onward journey: a mid-morning, inter-city train to Doncaster.

I have a lie-in for the first time in ages. But guilt soon drags me out of bed and into action. I need to get a birthday card for my friend Christine and deliver it by 'gloved' hand at a safe distance on her West Ealing doorstep. I've been giving her the same birthday present for the past decade at least. A year's membership of Kew Gardens. We've both made good use of our membership over the years. Last year I didn't get there that often because of being on tour, but in a normal year I suppose I visit about twice a month. But who knows when we might be able to make use of it this year? If at all. And when we do, what might be the restrictions? Just when I have time at my disposal, Covid has closed Kew down: its gates, Lion, Victoria and Elizabeth, bar all-comers; and not just visitors, but many staff and volunteers too.

CHAPTER 2
"APRIL IS THE DEADLIEST MONTH"

Like Christine, I also have a spring birthday. 6th April. The start of the financial year. I was born at the end of the severe winter of 1947. I made a late appearance on the evening of Easter Sunday. There was still snow on the ground outside Mount Pleasant Hospital, Swansea. Perhaps the unseasonably cold weather was the reason for my refusal to leave the warmth of the womb. My dad wasn't best pleased as he missed out on a year's tax relief. If only I'd arrived a day earlier he would have qualified. There was a lot of teasing from his workmates apparently.

6th April 2020 is a Monday. Monday, a notoriously difficult day if you want to ensure the prompt delivery of birthday cards. Mine have been arriving in a trickle over a few days, so by the day itself there are about thirty to open. Not a bad haul considering it's not a significant birthday, and in the circumstances. However, for the first time ever I'm forced to make my own birthday cake as there's no one to buy or bake for me. I dust off Nicola Sloane's excellent recipe

for Lemon Drizzle which she gave to me when we were both at The Palladium in *The Sound of Music*. (Clang!)

We played opposite each other as Frau Schmidt, the housekeeper, and Franz, the butler. Years before we had worked together in a production of *The Gondoliers* at the Bristol Old Vic and had a great rapport on and off stage.

Madame Sloane's
Amazing Lemon Drizzle Cake

For the cake

- 6oz/175g margarine (soft)
- 6oz/175g caster sugar
- 6oz/175g self-raising flour
- 3 eggs
- grated rind of 2 lemons

For the drizzle

- 4oz/110g granulated sugar
- juice of the two lemons

Method

- Grease a loose-bottomed deep round cake tin (7"/18cm) and line with baking parchment, which you also grease. In a clean mixing bowl cream the marg and sugar with a handheld electric whisk until the mixture is light and fluffy. Beat in the eggs one at a time. Stir in the lemon zest. Sift the flour and fold into the mixture gradually with a metal tablespoon.
- Turn into the lined tin and bake in a moderate oven – Gas Mark 3/160 C – for an hour, until the cake springs back when pressed with a finger.
- Meanwhile, mix granulated sugar and lemon juice. Remove cake from tin and peel off paper. Skewer holes over the top. Stand cake on a wire rack above a dinner plate and spoon over the topping. Keep tipping the excess from the plate and go back over the top!

I have been known to cut the cake in half horizontally and spread the bottom with homemade lemon curd and then sandwich together, working on the principle that more is moreish, but it's my birthday and I'm not looking for work. So I stick in three candles, one for each year over seventy, light them, sing happy birthday to me in Welsh, blow them out, make a wish and tuck into a generous slice. Moist, sweet, sharp and light. A real treat. But one I can't share. I think it's a bit dodgy to offer my cake to the neighbours, as much as I'd like to, so I pop the rest ready-sliced in the freezer for a week of subsequent spoilings. Later, after I've eaten my solitary supper, Pip and Tommy knock. Having seen the steady stream of envelopes over the last week, they have rightly guessed it's my birthday and have some cake for me, and a chorus. I don't have the heart to say I've baked my own, and put the Sainsbury's special into a cake tin for future naughtiness.

A few days later I see our postie, Stacey, and thank him for being so efficient during the pandemic in making sure we've received our mail each day as usual, adding I'm particularly grateful that all my birthday cards arrived in time. His reply is typical of his upbeat attitude: "Just doing my job. I'm lucky: at least I still have one!"

As I'm one of the 'unlucky' ones I suppose I could be forgiven for indulging in some self-pity. But what's the point? Nobody likes a moaner. And I am better off than most. Of course I can't help thinking about the *craic* I would have had during my birthday week in Cork with the *Mousetrap* company, and my friends, Gaynor, Nick and Lyndall, who had all planned on coming over for a few days. As the beautiful spring weather settles in for a lengthy spell, I count my blessings and write a poem expressing this sentiment. The opening line is a parody of the first from Robert Browning's 'Home Thoughts, from Abroad', "Oh, to be in England…"

Oh, to be in Cork

If I'd been in Cork, I'd have missed:
Magnolia leaning over my fence,
pink and blousy;
Planting Daniel Deronda in his new bed,
budding, full of hope;
My neighbour's cherry tree
wearing its Easter bonnets;
The Sun new on my back
as I sow my salad seeds;
The songs of birds and bees,
and the soft silence in between.
I would have missed
This Spring.
So, for now,
Cork can wait:
I'll be back anon.

14th April

I turn a few more thoughts into words today. Yes, the old-fashioned way with pen and paper. It takes the form of a five-line poem. Is there a word for that I wonder? I think it might be a quintain. So here it is:

B.C. (a quintain for quarantine)

> First there was Brexit;
> It drove us all apart.
> Then came Corona;
> It brought us back together –
> Two metres – but it's a start!

On impulse, totally out of character and contrary to previous behaviour, I decide to post it on Facebook. It is met with a hundred responses: a mix of thumbs-up, hearts and comments. That's social media for you, I guess.

21st April

Inevitable I suppose that reading a new prayer each day would lead me to pen one of my own:

Prayer for Today

> Oh, Lord, look down on London in lockdown.
> Amen.

When this is posted on FB I get a few 'Amens' and a 'God Bless'. Lots of the likes and comments are from friends I haven't heard from in years. Perhaps there is something to be said for this new-to-me public platform after all? I make a promise that I won't use it as a political soapbox. Surely that misses the point. This is not a time for ranting.

23rd April

Two anniversaries coincide today. St George's Day and Shakespeare's birthday. Shakespeare was born 456 years ago.

My earliest memory of Shakespeare happened in an unlikely setting: not at the theatre, not in school, but on a Sunday evening in Chapel when I was about ten or eleven. The preacher that night quoted from *The Tempest*, though I had no idea of that at the time: "We are such stuff As dreams are made on, and our little life Is rounded with a sleep."

Pure genius. Simple yet profound. I've never forgotten the tingling sensation on first hearing those words.

I think it would have been a couple of years later when we began to study him at school. The play was *Macbeth*, a fitting choice for teenage boys. I was struck by its breathless pace, its power, its language, and its close examination of the destructive, lethal force of ruthless ambition. When I reach the sixth form, English is one of my three chosen subjects for A Level. Sadly, we don't do any acting in our Comp; but a mile across the boggy common, in Mynyddbach School for Girls, it's a different story. The pupils mount a production of 'the Scottish Play'. My friend Veronica is unrecognisable, convincing and compelling in the eponymous role. I'm impressed.

Go easy with the bat-spit, dear!

A week or so later I go to Bishop Gore School and see their production of *King Lear*. The title role is played by a charismatic eighteen-year-old called Gareth Armstrong. The two prodigies pass these stiff tests brilliantly. Nearly sixty years on, both of them are still my close friends. Indeed, it was Gareth's production of *The Mousetrap* that I was touring when Covid made all theatres dark this March.

I think I discovered Shakespeare's Sonnets around the age of sixteen. A perfect age to identify with their intense passions: feelings of love, joy, despair, grief, insecurity, jealousy, loss, mortality. The first one I learned by heart was 'Sonnet 18'. That was the choice for today from my constant Corona companion: *A Poem for Every Night of the Year* (this, a recent birthday gift from my Mumbles chums, Cecily and Bob Hughes. A perfect partner for *A Poem for Every Day of the Year*.)

I digress. Oh, yes, 'Sonnet 18'. You'll be familiar with it I'm sure. It starts with a question…

Shall I compare thee to a summer's day?

…contains the memorable, and often-quoted…

Rough winds do shake the darling buds of May…

…and ends with the unshakable affirmation of a faithful lover and supremely confident poet:

So long as men can breathe or eyes can see,
So long lives this, and this gives life to thee.

That's quite some love letter.

Now from the sublime to the…!

An offering of my own in honour of the Swan of Avon:

Shakespeare in Confinement

When Will came out of quarantine
He brought King Lear *with him.*
What will we come out with,
Apart from longer hair?

A different take on things perhaps?

In these days I think it's wise to keep our Shakespeare close.

Apart from my daily walk and the weekly doorstep clap for the NHS, I'm not going out much these days. However, I'm still keen on keeping up appearances. There's not much I can do about my hair. Fortunately, I had it cut during our week in Leicester last month so it's not too unruly yet. But I don't see much point in shaving. I'll grow a lockdown beard, though I will keep it neatly trimmed. When it comes to shirts I'm not going to drop my standards. I shall carry on ironing, if only for my own satisfaction. I record my fastidiousness in a short poem: a haiku. And a pun.

"Still ironing shirts?"
"If I look good: I feel good;
So I'll just press on!"

27th April

In the early days of the outbreak when it was confined to China, it seemed a distant threat. We kept calm and carried on. Working, and living life to the full. When it reached Italy we began to take it seriously. Too close for comfort. News of the spread started to dominate news bulletins and all of our waking hours. It kept us awake at night. A few weeks into the outbreak my friend and colleague Susie Penhaligon turned to me over morning coffee and said: "Johnnie, have you seen what Covid looks like under the microscope? It's actually quite beautiful."

I thought it not unlike a psychedelic mushroom: a fatal fungus. I put this in epigram form:

Pretty Deadly

> *Up close, Covid-19's quite a looker:*
> *It really takes your breath away.*

28th April

The poem for today is 'Desiderata'.

I hadn't read it for years. There was a time when it was everywhere: on greetings cards, plaques, plates, even tea towels. Overfamiliarity had made it hackneyed and stale. But reading it again made me think it is so right for now when we have time to reflect and ask the deeper questions that often our busy schedules push to one side. I quote a short extract here that hit the mark:

> *Take kindly the counsel of the years…*
> *Do not distress yourself with dark imaginings.*
> *Many fears are born of fatigue and loneliness…*
> *Therefore be at peace with God,*
> *whatever you may conceive Him to be,*
> *and whatever your labours and aspirations,*
> *in the noisy confusion of life,*
> *keep peace with your soul.*

29th April

A Time to Dance
I was ready to pass on a newly penned ode today when I

discover that it's International Dance Day. I come across a funny and thoughtful poem called 'Dancing with Life' by Shauna Darling Robertson. What a great name.

Many of my musical theatre chums will laugh at my paying homage to dance, as out of the triple threat of Acting, Singing and Dancing, I've always found the latter discipline to be the toughest. I would like to apologise retrospectively to the dance partners I've crippled over the years. I must have driven the two. Miss Gillies – Gregory and Lynne – to distraction, though they never gave up on me. One of the proudest moments of my career was on the opening night of *The Sound of Music* at the London Palladium when Arlene Phillips awarded me a "10" for my Viennese Waltz. All right, it was a joke: she gave them to all the cast; but still, I was chuffed to bits. Enough name-dropping. (Clang!) Shauna's poem comes from her collection, *Saturdays at the Imaginarium* (Troika 2020) and is included with kind permission. Wait for it… 5,6,7,8…

Dancing with Life

> *I beckoned to the floor*
> *missed buses and lost races.*
> *We body-popped till sore.*
>
> *I held out my hand*
> *to every failed exam.*
> *We lindy-hopped. We can-canned.*
> *I slipped my arm around the waist*

of Chicken! Loser! Nerd!
We skip-jived at a pace.

I chose the longest, dullest week
and pressed it to my chest
as we cha-cha'd cheek to cheek.

I tipped and doffed my hat
to a hundred horrid haircuts.
We mambo'd, tango'd, tapped.

Feeling bold, I turned to face
my darkest, rawest faults.
I took them in my arms, we bowed
and broke into a waltz.

30th April

Lord, How Long?

Quarantine: it must be over, surely? I've just used my last teabag, and I know there were forty when I started isolating. At the outset I was clean-shaven, having removed Major Metcalf's moustache when the run of the play was suspended. Now I have a full beard.

If other proof were needed, I've reached Psalm 40 in my daily reading.

So it's true, that's how long lockdown has lasted. The equivalent of Noah's flood or the desert retreat of Jesus.

The first verse of Psalm 40 reads:

I waited patiently for the Lord: He inclined unto me.

We will have to wait a while longer yet I fear. Like the psalmist we must be patient. Not easy. But this too will pass.

I bring to mind Daniel Defoe's masterpiece, *Robinson Crusoe*. When it was published in 1719, novels were 'new'. Hence 'novel'. Because Defoe gave the author as 'Robinson Crusoe', many readers believed it to be an autobiography. They weren't familiar with novels after all.

In a clever nine-line poem, Ian McMillan imagines what wise sayings Crusoe might have come up with. I came up with one of my own:

How Long?

I wonder how long this beard should be?
After forty days, I think it's long enough.

CHAPTER 3
"ROUGH WINDS DO SHAKE THE DARLING BUDS OF MAY"

1st May

May Day! May Day!
A double meaning.
    I know which I prefer.

2nd May

Nothing New
The Blame game is not new.

Historians claim the Black Death was brought back by a merchant ship, returning from the East to Genoa, Northern Italy in 1492. The same year that Columbus landed in the

Caribbean.Over the following centuries, traders and invaders took pathogens from the Old World to the New. And as the conquerors and colonisers spread, so did disease. They came bearing gifts: cholera, typhoid, smallpox and measles.

Move on four centuries and a worldwide influenza pandemic wiped out nearly fifty million. It's been labelled 'Spanish Flu', unfairly as it happens. In fact it didn't originate in Spain at all. As that country was neutral during the First World War it had no news blackout and so reporting of the outbreak wasn't subject to censorship. The Spanish called it 'French Flu', which was probably more accurate. It's likely that the virus thrived in the insanitary conditions in the trenches, and was spread unwittingly by men returning from the Front.

Wars, invasions, global trade and international travel all come at a cost.

I write a poem on the theme...

A Word in Marco Polo's Ear

This time you've gone too far.
All right, I know you brought us noodles:
and they slipped down easily.

Don't get me wrong,
we're not ungrateful for the rice either.
We love the feel of silk against the skin,
and the tickle of spice in our noses
and on our tongues.

But Marco,
my only gripe with you
is this:
Why,
Oh, why,
did you bring us
This
back from China?

3rd May

Salisbury Cathedral at 800

Today we commemorate the 800th anniversary of Salisbury Cathedral. It hasn't always occupied its present site. The previous Norman church stood in Old Sarum which by the thirteenth century was becoming an increasingly unsuitable location for such a prestigious building. A rotten borough indeed.

Papal blessing was sought and granted to move the old cathedral, stone by stone, a couple of miles south to a new and blessed spot: a water meadow where five rivers meet. The foundation stone was laid in 1220, and within a generation the new cathedral arose. This miracle was achieved in thirty-eight years by a devoted legion of masons, carpenters and glaziers.

As a result it is the only English cathedral built in one style. The finest example of early English gothic. Its crowning glory was soon to follow: an elegant spire, the tallest at that time in Europe: 123 metres; a stat that every self-respecting

Russian agent learns these days at Putin's knee. In the thirteenth century it would, of course, have been measured in feet.

Inside, it houses the oldest working clock in the world, dating from c.1386; and a copy of Magna Carta, the best-preserved of the four which survive.

The Welsh-born seventeenth-century poet, orator, priest and hymn-writer George Herbert thought the Cathedral and its surrounding Close to be the nearest one can get to Heaven on earth. And the artist Constable admired the view so much that he painted it no fewer than six times.

If Herbert were alive today he might well celebrate the occasion by writing:

Today, on this day of days,
Accept, oh, Lord, the song we raise,
And this, our sacrifice of praise.

I have a strong connection with and affection for Salisbury. I have appeared at the Playhouse in two productions, playing the Judge in Sweeney Todd and my first pantomime dame, Sarah the Cook in Dick Whittington. But nothing can compare with my last theatrical experience in the city. This was not in the Playhouse but in the nave of the Cathedral, on Good Friday 2003, when I performed for the last time my one-man show, *The Gospel According to John*, to some 600 souls. An occasion I shall never forget and which, on this special day, seems fresher than ever.

Good Friday, 2003

> *Six hundred sit in darkness.*
> *The music rests.*
> *Silence.*
> *Three knocks.*
> *And the oak door,*
> *its old joints complaining loudly,*
> *opens to the night,*
> *then shuts.*
> *A candle splits the dark…*
> *"In the beginning"*
> *All hear the Word*
> *made fresh.*

4th May

Leisure

I'm a great admirer of W.H. Davies. He was a tramp as well as a poet. Mr Ede, the deputy head at my secondary school, introduced me to 'Leisure' – Davies' most famous poem – in the early sixties. I've loved it ever since. It will be familiar to many because it features in an advert for Center Parks. There's an echo of the opening and closing lines of the poem, "A poor life this if, full of care,
We have no time to stand and stare" in my piece which follows:

A Man of Leisure

> *This morning I lay in a deep-filled bath*
> *For fully half an hour.*
> *I find it gives me time to think;*
> *Far better than a shower.*
> *What is this life if, full of care,*
> *We don't make time to lie in there?*

5th May

Birds in Brilliant Brentford

I moved to 'Brentford-Upon-Thames', as the estate agent would have it, in December 2011. On my first night in Mafeking Avenue I remember collapsing into my new bed, late and exhausted, and before dropping off, saying to myself: "I'm going to be happy here."

And so it has proved. *Brentford is brilliant*, but how it has changed in the intervening years. It is hardly recognisable. So many homes and businesses have sprung up, and two major developments are underway: the southern side of the High Street has been knocked down as part of The Brentford Project, and Brentford Football Club – 'The Bees' – was due to leave its old home, Griffin Park, at the end of the season for a brand-new, state-of-the-art stadium a mile to the east, next to Kew Bridge Station.

Both these plans are on hold at the moment. That's true for lots of us as we're confined to our homes during lockdown...

But not so for the birds: they are busy building. They seem to be relishing the clearer skies and quieter streets. And as they work and mate and make their nests in our now nature-friendly gardens, they sing, louder than ever it seems. But that's because the competition has piped down, I reckon. We listen with growing wonder and respect.

The not-so-busy-bird

All the birds are busy
and in full voice this Spring.
All bar one, that is:
the crane is standing still.

6th May

The Sound of Silence

When friends visit me for the first time, they often comment how quiet our street is "for London". Compared to some parts of the metropolis, I suppose it is. However, some days we are under the flight path of planes coming in to land at Heathrow. They can start as early as 5.00am, and as many as forty an hour can fly over Brentford, which is not ideal. Not at the moment, of course. I can't remember when I last heard a plane … and there, bang on cue, and just to contradict me, one passes, but not directly overhead. A distant, muffled rumble. In two months Heathrow has gone from 600 landings a day to sixty. I find myself conflicted about Heathrow expansion and the building of another runway. Surely it will inevitably lead to busier skies, more noise and increased pollution? But at the moment we city-dwellers can relish the sound of silence while it lasts. Many of us are taking advantage of the silence to have meaningful, quiet times. Mindfulness, negating stress, and leading to peace and calm.

Behind Locked Doors

> *Today is so quiet,*
> *I swear I can hear,*
> *Behind the wardrobe door,*
> *A moth,*
> *Masticating.*

8th May

102 Not Out

My friend Alf Thomas is 102 not out today. Below is a tribute to him: a small token of my respect, admiration and affection for a remarkable man. His mind is as sharp as ever, and he's still up for a lively discussion on current affairs. Alf has always been a political animal with a strong sense of social justice, and has served his community with unflinching commitment for eighty years in all parts of Swansea, from Manselton to Mumbles via Fforestfach. *Da iawn*. Well done, Alf. *Penblwydd hapus!* Happy birthday!

102 Not Out

Alf, you're in the First Eleven.
You've reached 102 not out.
Spanish Flu failed to bowl you over,
And now you'll see Corona off as well.
Your eye is in.
Steady now
Old friend:
This one's a googly.
Ready now?
Knock it
for six

What is Alf's secret to longevity, I wonder? I don't bother to ask him because I know he'll just say: "Well, actually, I've been very lucky and have a lot to be thankful for."

I think the answer lies in a combination of:

A positive outlook. Strong principles. Hard work. A refusal to join the rat race. And our hero's a non-smoker, a moderate drinker, and a vegetarian. But don't get the wrong idea. He's not a killjoy. He's great fun and jolly good company.

9th May

Her Majesty
Who can fail to have been impressed and moved by the Queen's broadcast last night? Simply and sincerely, she

managed once again to hit the right note. Whatever we are going through at the moment – and it is hellish – we should not forget what our country, the Commonwealth, our allies and the world suffered for six harrowing years of war, not to mention the utter depravity of the Holocaust. How reassuring it was yesterday to listen to Her Majesty and get her perspective on things. After all, she had first-hand experience of the Second World War. Her words of wisdom carried weight.

Before I sign off, I'd like to pass on a personal memory. It concerns my mother – our Eileen. For the last eight years of her life she suffered with vascular dementia, and received exemplary care at St Martin's Home in Swansea. On one of my visits in 2012, I brought the conversation round to the Queen's Diamond Jubilee.

The chat went like this:

"Mam, do you remember where we were when we heard that the King had died?"

"No."

"Well, we were sitting in Aunty Betty's front room: her, you, the corgi and me, when John Snagge, I think it was, came on the wireless, and said: 'The King is dead.'"

"You've got an amazing memory for a man of seventy-nine!"

"But, Mam, I'm only sixty-five."

"Fancy."

Then after a moment's reflection, she added:

"You know, I love the Queen. What a remarkable woman. Sixty years on the *phone*."

10th May

Mother's Day

Today is Mother's Day in Canada, Australia and the USA. Here in the UK we stole a *March* on them and marked it two months ago. Old fogeys like me still insist on calling it 'Mothering Sunday'. Part of the tradition was the gift of flowers, usually violets; they arrive early in spring and speak of love.

The maternal bond is strong: a love like no other. Today I salute the mothers I know or have known from those three far-flung countries…

I remember *Rosemary George*, my childhood sweetheart, who married Stephen Waterhouse, settled with him in British Columbia, raised her children, and then was snatched away too soon…

I think of *Jane Atkinson* in Perth, Western Australia: a brilliant mum to Josh and Ben through the toughest of challenges…

And *Joan Chambers* in Melbourne. Her two are now adults. She passed on her love of the arts to Alex and Steve, and how they have flourished.

I still feel the loss of my cousin Dorothy who met David Prairie, an American, at a wedding in Canada, fell for him, left her beloved Wales, married him, moved to Illinois and gave him the precious gifts of Jeremy, Caroline and Nathan. She loved and lived for her children. Cruelly taken from them by meningitis over twenty years ago.

But, on a happier note: a story of survival.

Today I want to congratulate another special mother: my

cousin Jill, who, just like her sister Dorothy, fell for a Yank. In fact she did it a few years before her younger sibling. Her beau was Mick Hardley, and after marriage they moved to Michigan, leaving behind in Swansea not just her family, but also a string of broken-hearted suitors. Jill was a stunner. Think Catherine Zeta-Jones in *Darling Buds of May* and you get the idea.

When Jill's two youngest – Amanda and Steve – were still babies, her own mother died. Returning to the States after the funeral in Swansea must have been hard. But Jill is a fighter. She recovered from polio as a child, and perhaps this early setback prepared her to face down all that life has thrown at her since. She is now the proud matriarch of the Hardley clan, and has formed alliances with the Foresters, the Hamiltons and even a family called Jones – those Welsh get everywhere. That she is still flourishing is testament to her strength of character, her unshakeable Christian faith and her unfailing sense of humour. She is one of the funniest people you could meet. A natural comedienne.

Jill, my lovely girl, if you were here now, I would give you a crushing cwtch[1], and when you had got your breath back, I would cook you the full Swansea breakfast: sausage, bacon, egg, cockles and laverbread – your favourite. God bless you and keep you and yours safe.

All my love.

Cousin John. x.

---

1   *Cwtch* – a Welsh dialect word that can mean the cupboard under the stairs or a warm embrace: half cuddle, half hug. There's a saying: "Anyone can hug, but only the Welsh can *cwtch*." You'll have to wait until Covid has passed to find out if it's true.

11th May

Mr Pope: A Man of God

In the midst of the VE day celebrations this weekend, I received some sad news: Stan Pope, one of the nicest men I ever knew, had died in Swansea at the age of 97. At such a time, people often say: "He'll be sorely missed." It's become a cliché. In this case it is certainly true. Stan was a one-off: intelligent, caring, warm, engaging and kind. He was a dedicated teacher and one of the finest preachers I ever heard. His sermons were inspiring, always beautifully constructed and delivered with burning conviction. His lilting Pontrhydyfen accent, a delight to the rapt listener. Often he would include personal details of his early life in that Afan valley village to illustrate a point, or share experiences of his time in the Navy. How poignant that this ex-serviceman should pass on such a significant Second World War anniversary.

His whole life was spent in service to his family, his friends, his pupils, his rose garden, his Assembly, his community, his country, but most of all to his Lord. I cherish so many memories of him. On our last meeting I read the following story, in which Stan is mentioned, to him and his lovely wife Meudwen.

At the end he said:

"*Diolch yn fawr*. Thank you, brother John. Now let us have a word of prayer…"

Whitsun Teas

When I was a boy growing up in post-war Swansea, we didn't have a Spring Bank Holiday: it hadn't been invented. This was still the age of Chapel – three times on a Sunday and once in the week to Band of Hope. The holiday that followed six weeks after Easter was called Whitsun. On Whit Monday all the Sunday School, along with parents, teachers and the superintendent – the aptly named Mr Pope – would pack into a South Wales Transport double-decker bus bound for the seaside. One year it might be Llangennith; another, Llanmadoc. But by far the most favoured and favourite destination was Llansteffan.

Llansteffan was fabulous. It had everything children loved: a ruined castle perched high on a hill; a wild wood; fields full of grazing sheep and lambs; miles of golden sands; and, best of all, jellyfish, washed up by the high tide, and left stranded at low tide for curious young Charles Darwins to kick or poke with sticks, never brave enough to pick them up.

Then, back indoors for tea; a tea of teas. The best tea of the year. We stood behind our chairs, eager to tuck in, but waiting for grace, the signal to start...

"For what we are about to receive, may the Lord make us truly thankful. Amen."

The trestle tables were bowing with the food overload. There were pyramids of sandwiches, their neat triangles bursting with treasures: ham and mustard; cheese and tomato; and salmon, tinned, not fresh, but John West's best. Then, having left a tad of room for something sweet, we saw off the challenge of cream slices, chocolate éclairs and custard tarts.

And after that, though we could barely move, there were the races: sack, egg-and-spoon, three-legged and wheelbarrow. If it was raining – and this is West Wales we're talking about – these races took place in the Memorial Hall, kindly lent. But if the sun shone, the races, and the games of rounders that inevitably ensued, were held on the Sands.

On the way back on the bus there was singing:

Now Zaccheus was a very little man
And a very little man was he.
He climbed up into a sycamore tree,
For he wanted the Lord, to see.
And when the Saviour passed that way
He looked up into the tree,
And said:
"Zaccheus, you come down,
For I'm coming to your house for tea!"

"Hey, while we're on the subject, it's been a long time since tea. I'm starving."

"Perhaps we'll stop for chips."

"Or Joe's ice cream. That's the best."

And then, last of all, passing the hat round for the driver, Mr Williams, adding our leftover pennies to the collection.

"Fair play, he's been brilliant. Let's hope we get him next year."

"Yes, and that it's Llansteffan again."

"Good night."

"God bless."

12th May

"I name this child…"

Today marks the 200th anniversary of Florence Nightingale's birth. All of us learned at school how she served with distinction during the Crimean War and revolutionised nursing methods. She was ahead of her time, stressing the importance of hand-washing, and spacing out beds on the wards to avoid the spread of infections. An early example of social distancing. She had a holistic approach and catered for the emotional and spiritual needs of her patients as well as their physical injuries and conditions. Her sense of duty was rooted in her strong Christian faith.

I feel sure the popularity of the name Florence in the late nineteenth century was due to the respect in which she was held. Come to think of it, my grandparents, Dan and Fan Griffiths, called their first-born Florence, and I feel sure it must have been in her honour. In the twentieth century she was the first female figure to be featured on the back of our banknotes: the famous representation of her on her rounds, 'The Lady with the Lamp'. And now, during this pandemic, further recognition has come with the naming of the emergency hospitals after her.

It was very moving that when our prime minister, Boris Johnson, recovered from Covid, he and Carrie gave their son the name, among two others, of 'Nicholas' after the two doctors who, along with the nursing staff, had saved the prime minister's life. Sadly, some doctors have not been as lucky as Boris, and have paid the ultimate sacrifice in caring for others. We salute them on International Nurses' Day:

Lalaine, Jennie, John, Michael, Fiona, Elvira, Glen, Angie, Thomas, Liz... the list is long and growing. More will be added before this disease is quelled. Perhaps many more grateful parents will honour these contemporary heroes by naming a child after one of them. Some of these children might join this noble calling when they grow up. One thing is certain: we are always going to need health practitioners.

Let's hope we value them more in the future. And pay them accordingly.

13th May

It's Back

Yes, it's official: I heard it on Radio 4, so it must be right. We are all reading poetry as if it's going out of fashion. In fact, it had gone out of fashion, and was neglected for many years. Well, now it's back, and it's everywhere, on everyone's lips.

I've been reading a poem every morning and another at night; looking up some old friends, and being introduced to some new ones, too.

Among the favourites: Kipling, A.A. Milne, Oscar Wilde, W.H. Davies, John Clare, Thomas Hardy, Yeats.

And numbered among my new-found 'friends': Billy Collins, Kit Wright, Evan Jones and Shauna Darling Robertson.

Each day as well I make time to catch my friend Eleanor McLeod reading three of her own published poems for her young viewers, but this old codger loves them too, not to mention her colourful, coordinated outfits. A feast for the eye as well as the ear.

Poetry comes in all shapes and sizes, from the cheeky limerick to the lofty epic poem; and it can suit all moods and tastes. Some bards have experimented with *shape* verses. There's the clever punning poem, 'The Mouse's Tale' by Lewis Carroll; Dylan Thomas's daring experiment with form in 'Vision and Prayer'; but perhaps most stunning of all, is the brilliant symmetry of 'The Swan' by John Hollander. A creation of breathtaking beauty.

Poetry can distil the delights of the seasons as they pass; celebrate anniversaries; record events, public and personal, momentous or slight; and transport us to other worlds. We can lose ourselves, but find meaning at the same time. That's what it's doing for me during the current crisis.

Some days I write as well as read. Not so much a diversion, more an immersion. During the recent warm weather I've been charmed by a family who live over the fence, beyond the back lane at the bottom of my garden. There's always something going on: tons of laughter, some tears. Lots of noise. Loving, caring, intimate family noise. Grandma coaxing; father organising; older sister scaling walls, and when she catches my eye, shouting a friendly greeting; the toddler finding his voice and giving it full rein. I hear snatches of their conversation, not because I'm eavesdropping, but because I'm embraced warmly by their voices. I've transcribed one of the toddler's outbursts into a haiku, a Japanese three-line verse of seventeen syllables, organised, 5-7-5.

Be kind: the boy is young…
I've called it:

Mum's Working from Home

> *"Mummy, please be nice.*
> *Come downstairs: it's warm outside,*
> *And I want to play."*

14th May

Dylan Day

Today is International Dylan Thomas Day, and marks the first public recital of *Under Milk Wood* on 14th May 1953. That was in New York. Now his works are known and loved all over the world.

I was asked yesterday how I would mark the anniversary. Here goes…

I had my first cuppa of the day in my Dylan Thomas mug. His signature is on it, as well as a quote from his poem, 'In my Craft or Sullen Art'.

Then I recorded 'Dear Gwalia', the morning prayer from *Under Milk Wood*, for a friend in lockdown in Mumbles.

Now I'm posting this.

Below I will add 'Aunty Audrey's Sofa', one of the thirteen chapters from my solo piece: *Chapel, Chums and Chips: A Boy's Eye-view of Swansea Folk*.

And finally, this evening, just before turning off my bedside lamp, I will recite Eli's sunset poem.

A day packed with poetry.

(Here's a short piece I wrote a few years back about how I discovered Dylan!)

Aunty Audrey's Sofa

There I was sitting on my Aunty Audrey's sofa, next to my best friend, Aunty Audrey's dishy daughter Veronica, in front of the telly. Even though it was 1962, this was still a bit of a novelty for me, as we didn't have a TV at home: my parents didn't hold with it. As a result, whenever I got the chance to look at the Box, I seized it with both eyes. So here I was, glued to the snowy screen. And then it happened.

I sat up straight as I heard for the very first time those seismic words:

To begin at the beginning:
It is spring, moonless night in the small town, starless and
bible-black…

The force and freshness of those words blew me away; I very nearly fell off Aunty Audrey's sofa. For the next hour and three-quarters, though I wasn't counting, as time flew by like a winged horse with me riding on it, I was under the most powerful spell I had ever experienced. We neither of us spoke nor moved till well after the closing lines.

When we found words they came nowhere near to describing what we had just heard. Someone had written a play for *us* in the authentic, sing-song lingo of South West Wales. It was brash, it was blousy, it was bawdy, bucolic and beautiful beyond; and it was *ours*.

There was no time to lose. I had to get a copy of *Under Milk Wood* pronto; and had to find out more about this Dylan Thomas. Of course, I wasn't to know then how significant this, the first play ever written specifically for broadcast, was going to be in my life: as a student, as an amateur performer, as a teacher and ultimately as a professional actor. It's been a lucky play for me.

My first appearance in it was the Swansea Little Theatre's 1969 production. I made my professional debut in it at the Kenneth More, Ilford in 1977.

Happily there have been many subsequent performances:

Memorably on Radio 4 in the BBC's 25th Anniversary broadcast; and many others in the intervening years in places as far-flung as Kuwait, Kumasi, Canada; and nearer home on the shores of Lough Graney, County Clare; in the opening gala of the Millennium Centre, Cardiff; and at the Questors Theatre; but, most thrilling of all, as Mog Edwards in the National Theatre's production.

On the first night, as I ran up Llareggub Hill, level with the Dress Circle in the mighty Olivier, I felt on top of the world:

Beloved Myfanwy Price, my Bride in Heaven.

And I was. In heaven, I mean. Thank you, Aunty Audrey. I owe you a lot. Xxx

15th May

Barry Island and Porthcawl
I don't know if you, like me, have been enjoying the reruns of *Gavin and Stacey*. If anything, I love each episode more

the second time around. So I thought I'd share my own Barry Island tale with you today, but before I do, may I recommend, if you haven't already had the pleasure, Dylan Thomas's hilarious short story, 'The Outing', sometimes called 'The Trip to Porthcawl' – Barry's posher cousin.

The Sulphur of Hell

In Dylan's broadcast, 'Reminiscences of Childhood', two boys try to out-boast each other. Child A claims his father can afford to employ a chauffeur: B argues this is pointless as A's father hasn't got a car. Well, my father *was* a chauffeur, and he didn't have a car either. That is, until the sixties, when he bought an old Morris Minor from a workmate. Before then we would go on family holidays by train if it was up to London; by flat-bottomed steamer if it was across the choppy channel from Mumbles to Ilfracombe; but more often than not, Dad would buy a runabout ticket, which was valid for a week and which entitled you to unlimited bus travel all over South Wales. Usually, you knew where you were going, but sometimes the destination was a mystery. On one such trip, Mam and Dad (Eileen and Harold) left my brother Steve and me behind, and set off on a sunny Saturday evening by coach. Quite by chance they met up with Margaret and Beth, two spinster sisters from our Chapel. They were very devout, and took their religious convictions to extremes: no alcohol, no wireless, no newspapers, no TV. No men. Of all places, the destination turned out to be Barry Island with its tacky fairground – all 'kiss me quick' and candyfloss. As they were getting off the coach, Margaret, the elder and more disapproving sister, hunched her shoulders, gripped her

Bible, and with a sharp intake of breath, turned on my father as if he were to blame for this nightmare scenario:

"I can smell the Sulphur of Hell, Harold."

"Don't be silly, Margaret. That's the hot-dog stall!"

16th May

Food for Thought

I come from a family of foodies. I learned from an early age that whereas some people might eat to live, we lived to eat. But I think I might have mentioned that before.

The only time my parents were summoned to see my head teacher was in primary school when I refused to eat the school dinners because they fell short of the standard of cooking I had come to expect at home. My mother had learned to cook under the watchful eye of Miss Alice when she went into service in her teens. She was a wonderful

DAVID HARMER
2020

Mice are foodies too.

cook. But she wasn't the only one in the family to excel in the culinary arts. While her meringues and macaroons were beyond praise, her cousin Betty's *bara brith* (Welsh fruit loaf) and chocolate éclairs took some beating, while I never tasted better rice pudding or egg-custard tarts than those served up by Nana Griffiths.

17th May

Let the People Sing
Many will have been disappointed by the lack of the Eurovision Song Contest this year. We missed its silliness, its brashness and the blatantly biased, politically motivated voting. Last night's virtual alternative was a much calmer and less competitive affair, ABBA emerging as worthy winners with 'Waterloo', as the best of the best.

I'm sure I'm not alone in missing singing. Warbling in the bath, although raising the spirits and keeping the vocal chords in good health, is no substitute for the communal activity of singing with others or of performing live in front of an audience. Normal service will be resumed as soon as it is deemed safe. Germany is exiting from lockdown faster than most, but I think it's sad that, although places of worship were reopened last week, singing is strictly *verboten*. Apparently there is a higher risk of passing on the virus when we sing. I look forward to the time, not too distant I hope, when children will sing 'Morning has Broken' in school once more; churches will echo with psalms, hymns and anthems; choirs will practise and perform; and musical theatre in the

West End, across the country and around the world will attract the crowds again.

"Please Stand to Sing"

> *When the day comes,*
> *be ready*
> *Don't sit*
> *stand tall*
> *Sing loud*
> *Sing proud*
> *Don't sit down*
> *stand*
> *and rock the boat.*

18th May

A Tale of Two Teachers

"I'd like a ticket for tonight, please."

"Sorry, love, but the performance is totally sold out. Has been for a year!"

"But I've just watched the matinee and I've got to see the show again. I'll stand."

And so for the second time that Saturday I was enthralled by *Guys and Dolls*, performed by Swansea Amateur Operatic Society at the Grand Theatre. I was hooked. A year later, in 1968, I auditioned and joined the 'Swansea Ams', as they were affectionately known. For the previous six months I'd been having singing lessons with Madame Hazel Squires, otherwise I would have had neither the courage to audition nor the technique to get through.

I lost touch with the society when I took up a teaching post in London in September 1970, and although in those early London years I did plenty of singing in church and with a Gilbert & Sullivan Society, it wasn't until 1974 that I met my second singing teacher. This encounter, as you'll discover, changed my life.

The teacher's name was Jean Millar. She died last year in her nineties. It was a great honour to deliver the eulogy at her funeral. My affection for her was deep, and my debt immeasurable. I reproduce an edited version of what I delivered on the day, here. I called it:

Thank You for the Music
Summertime and the living is easy…
The singing and the song were both sublime, but it seemed an incongruous, unseasonal choice as the occasion was a staff Christmas party at a North Acton primary school in the early seventies. As the final note died away, the room erupted into prolonged applause. When that abated I ran and hugged the soprano, my colleague and friend Mabel Cowley:

"I had no idea you could sing like that. Your voice is pure gold and your technique, faultless. You must have had lessons…"

"I have, and I still do."

"With whom?"

"Jean Millar."

"I must meet her and see if she'll teach me."

"I warn you now, she's very Yorkshire. Blunt and picky. You'd have to audition."

A few months later, in the spring of '74, I made my way to 23, Redcliffe Square for the first time. After brief introductions I began my audition piece:

O, Isis and Osiris guide them,
Send down thy blessing on the pair…

I finished. A pause.

"Interesting. What is singing?"

"Well… I… um… er…"

"Well, I'll tell you what it's not. It's not just the making of beautiful sounds: it's telling a story through the medium of music, and runs through a whole range of emotions. Now, sing it again, and emphasise the meaning…"

And so my studies with Jean began.

She had impressive letters after her name: ARCM; LRAM. But the qualifications are only part of the story. Jean had the gift of getting to the heart of a song and getting the best out of the singer. Added to that, she was a sensitive, supportive accompanist. She never referred to her days as a performer, or why her promising career was cut short. What disappointment she might have felt did not manifest itself in any signs of bitterness or regret, and she threw herself into teaching with gusto. It was never second best.

However tired one might have been feeling at the start of a lesson after a hard day's work, an hour's study with Jean was a tonic. One left the flat in Earl's Court refreshed, uplifted, encouraged.

On a personal note: I know I would never have made the step from primary school teacher to professional performer if it hadn't been for the confidence she instilled and the skills she passed on...

So, thank you, Jean; and *thank you for the music*, for giving it to me.

23rd May

Operetta and Rounders
My musical education started long before I met Hazel Squires and Jean Millar: way back in Cadle Junior School in the 1950s. Singing had a prominent position in the syllabus thanks to an extraordinary music teacher with a very unusual name: Miss Culpick.

Blow the wind southerly,
Southerly, southerly,
Blow the wind...

"Quick. Sit down. Miss is coming!"
We always had advanced warning of Miss Culpick's approach as she and her song drifted along the long corridors of Cadle School. And she invariably was carrying a kettle, its lead trailing behind her, the attached plug adding occasional percussion as it hit the hard concrete floor. Seconds later, in she would breeze. She was what you might call a heavy contralto. And her touch on the piano keys was heavy, too. Anyway, that was my father's opinion. I thought Miss Culpick

could do no wrong and was upset when Dad said she should have taken her gloves off when she accompanied the choir in a concert.

Music was her bag. I don't remember the three Rs being prioritised in her class. All we ever seemed to do was music; and music meant singing; and singing meant songs: dozens of them. And not just Welsh ones, though they were well represented, especially as the first of March approached. St David's Day. *Dydd Gwyl Dewi Sant*. A day of daffodils and leeks; and no lessons at all as every class joined in the morning-long *eisteddfod*. And then the whole of the pipe-hatted, lacy-shawled, leek-spitting, Welsh-flannelled afternoon off.

We must have covered other subjects from March to May, but as soon as the warmer weather came there was running, stool-ball, cricket in a bumpy field, and my favourite by far, rounders. I loved being the pitcher. Or the fielder at first base. I wasn't too good at fielding in the deep as my throwing was even worse than my batting. But that mattered not a hoot. I loved the game.

Towards the end of the summer term there were always two highlights: Annual Sports Day and the inter-house rounders tournament. I played for the Blues but I think the Reds always won.

After the six-week holiday there was the excitement of a new class teacher, another year and the rehearsals for the Christmas production to look forward to. A run-of-the-mill carol concert or a simple Nativity play were not ambitious enough for the staff and pupils of Cadle School. It had to be an operetta. I can't recall any of the titles, but I know they were lavish affairs involving singing, acting and dancing. I remember one year we went to a Madame Dunne to be taught the minuet. Her studio was in Gwydr Crescent up the Uplands, a posh part of town, especially to a lad who lived in a prefab on a council estate. Little wonder, after this early introduction to musical theatre, that I have felt so at home since in the works of Gilbert and Sullivan, Rogers and Hammerstein, Sondheim, Andrew Lloyd Webber et al.

It all started in Cadle Junior Mixed with Miss Culpick and a large cast, featuring: 'The Raggle-Taggle Gypsies'; 'Bobby Shafto'; 'David of the White Rock'; 'The Sweet Lass of Richmond Hill'; 'The Minstrel Boy'; 'My Grandfather's Clock'; 'Danny Boy'; 'The Men of Harlech'… and many, many more.

Now I've mentioned them, I'll be whistling, la-la-ing and humming them for days. If you know them, sing along too.

Songs are quite an education.

24th May

Holy Days on Hold
St Patrick started it. No, not the virus but the lockdown on 17th March. The usual riotous shenanigans were off limits, not only in the Republic but amongst the Irish Diaspora across the globe. That set the trend. *Passover* came and went with a whimper. *Easter*, too. Both these festivals with family at their hearts, and public worship. But not this year. Synagogues, churches, temples and mosques: all closed. The daily fasting during *Ramadan* was little changed, but not so the feasting with the family and friends at the end of the day.

Eid al-Fitr today was a muted affair. In all the brouhaha I'm sure we've missed Buddha's birthday and *Holi*, the Hindu celebration of spring.

In a few days' time, *Shavuot*, the Jewish festival of Weeks, will be the latest victim. How many more holy days will suffer neglect before we get back to normal and can enjoy them without fear or restraint? By the time we reach *All Saints* and *All Souls*, let's pray the pandemic will have passed, and that fireworks will explode with all their usual pyrotechnic exuberance at *Diwali*. Perhaps by *Hanukkah* and *Christmas* we will eventually emerge, blinking into the light, leaving the night behind, ready to face whatever the New Year will bring. Until then we have to hold on to three unfailing friends: **Faith, Hope** and **Love.**

25th May

On the Beet

Looking back at yesterday's entry I might well have added a fourth friend – food. Having read 'Food for Thought' on 16th May, you will already know that I love my grub. If I'm not eating it, I'm preparing it. Now I have a new project: growing it. To be precise: carrots, lettuce, tomatoes, rocket, basil and beetroot. I love beetroot but I know lots of people don't. Perhaps they were put off it in childhood. In the fifties it was the poor relation in many a soggy, vinegar-soused salad. Now it has been reinvented. When I see it in the local supermarket, bunched and blushing, I can't resist.

Boil it in salted water for about an hour, depending on

size. Or wrap individually in foil and bake in a moderate oven till tender. Of course it would take a third of the time and use less gas in a pressure cooker, but mine died. (Note to self: get a new one.)

Back to the beets. Test them with a skewer to see if they're done. Wait for them to cool a bit and then slip off the skins. Serve still warm as part of a meal, perhaps with the addition of crème fraiche or horseradish sauce.

Or try my friend Carole's suggestion and introduce it raw to the pot when cooking a beef casserole, which gives the dish added depth, colour and flavour. Freshly cooked beetroot combined with mature cheddar makes a delicious sandwich. Watching the carbs? Then try tossing beets in a salad with sliced orange, toasted hazelnuts, rocket and vinaigrette. Sometimes I cut cooked beets in half, top with a slice of goat's cheese, pop under the grill and then serve with fresh mint and a dressing of balsamic glaze or pomegranate molasses.

An actor friend, Richard Heffer, recommends a dish called 'Red Flannel'. All you do is add cubed beets to the classic corned beef hash. A veggie version which combines potato, onion, cabbage and beetroot is just as good.

My final suggestion for this burgundy beauty sounds bizarre, but, hand on heart, it's brilliant. Beetroot jelly. No, honestly. Give it a go. I passed it on to Anna Karen – Olive from *On the Buses* – when we appeared in *The Bed Before Yesterday* last century, and she's been making it ever since.

Beetroot Jelly

Put a kettle on to boil. Meanwhile break a raspberry jelly into cubes and pop into a Pyrex measuring jug. Pour on enough of the boiling water to cover the cubed jelly, about a third of a pint/190ml. Stir briskly until the jelly is completely dissolved. Then top up to a pint/570ml with red wine vinegar. Slice cooked beetroot into a sterilised jar and pour jelly over the top. Cool, seal and put into the fridge to set. It will keep in the fridge for a fortnight, but I can guarantee it won't last that long. Scrummy with cold cuts or cheese.

Today I see the seeds I sowed three weeks ago are sprouting.

In a couple of months I will be eating my own home-grown beetroot.

I can't wait.

26th May

Sparrow Grass
This is a rather common-or-garden moniker for the King of the Vegetable Kingdom: *Asparagus Officinalis* – to give its proper Latin title.

In days gone by it would have appeared exclusively on the tables of the well-to-do, but now it has become, if not exactly cheap, affordable; and one bunch can go a long way. There was a time when all of the domestically produced crop came from the Vale of Evesham, but now it's just as likely to have been grown in Cambridgeshire, Lincolnshire or Kent. Our home-grown variety has a short season that spans the three months from April to June, but at other times we import a staggering amount, mainly from Peru. I won't make a glib political point here, or take the moral high ground, but I don't want jet-lagged asparagus in December, just as I have no longing for strawberries out of season when they are oversized and have no flavour.

Asparagus has been eaten since Roman times. A recipe for it can be found in the world's oldest surviving cookbook:

Wash asparagus, rub it in a mortar, pour in water, filter through a strainer and throw away the fig-peckers. Grind six scruples of pepper and add two ladles of wine. Put three ounces of oil into a stockpot and boil. Stir six eggs into the asparagus and wine mixture. Cook and serve with more pepper. Don't try this at home.

There are ways with asparagus that I *can* endorse:

- You can steam, poach or bake it.
- You can wrap it up in prosciutto or dust it with parmesan.
- You can serve it swimming in melted butter or with a classic Hollandaise.
- Why not try it in risotto or in a pasta dish with broad beans and leeks?
- Or in a quiche with a mixture of cheddar and parmesan cheeses.
- How about in a stir-fry with chicken? A winning combination.

Last night I had half a bunch in a cheese omelette, mixing a little pesto in the eggs before cooking. The other half made a lovely light lunch with butter and pepper. The woody ends were broken off and made into soup with chicken stock. After blending it was passed through a sieve to remove the tough fibres. The bunch cost £1.50 and did three meals.

My absolute favourite way of eating these dreamy spears is with Jersey Royals, poached egg and some shavings of parmesan.

Enjoy it while it's still with us.

A Following Wind

After posting 'Sparrow Grass' on Facebook yesterday I received feedback from my friend Jonathan Ellis. He said I should have mentioned the side effects that can arise after eating asparagus. One is *wind*: the other *smelly pee*. With good reason it gained the nickname 'Chambermaid's Horror'. Say no more.

27th May

Rhubarb... Rhubarb... Rhubarb

Ever wondered why actors who are not involved directly in the action stand upstage in small groups and repeat the word 'rhubarb' ad infinitum? Apparently, from a distance it sounds like genuine conversation. The soft sounds of the word being preferable to the sibilance of 'celery' or the sharp consonants of 'carrot' or 'courgette', I suppose.

Rhubarb is at its very best just now, though its young

cousin, the upstart *forced* variety has been around since January. A word of warning if you've never cooked it before: *only the stalks are edible.* The leaves are highly *poisonous* and should *never* be eaten. Although it is technically a vegetable, it is treated like a fruit, and a tasty one at that.

If it's one of your favourites you will have your own ideas of how best to prepare and present it.

Delicious served simply with custard.

You can bake it in a pie, with or without a bottom.

Or as a cobbler or crumble. I think rhubarb fool takes some beating, especially if you have the time, and can find eggs and go to the bother of making it with real custard. Well worth the effort. I can recommend Delia Smith's version.

If you have the desire, the know-how and above all the patience to wait eight months, you could have a go at turning it into wine. May Bede, a delightful Devon lady I met in the seventies, had, at any one time, a thousand bottles of homemade wine in her Dulverton cellar. Dozens of the empties could be found drying outside, upturned on the spikes of the railings. May's mantra was:

"You can make wine out of anything, m'dear."

She was as good as her word and used tea, gooseberry, damson, elder – both the flowers and berries; even parsnip. But her *pièce de résistance* was rhubarb wine, a refreshing dry white which packed a punch.

My kind neighbour Mary got me two lots of rhubarb recently. There was enough to make crumble and a fool, but there was still some left over. So for breakfast I used it up in a compote with orange, ginger, honey, porridge oats and yoghurt. It got the day off to a cracking start I can tell you.

First I put two tablespoons of oats in a thick-bottomed pan and dry-fried them until golden brown, allowing them to cool slightly before stirring in a dessertspoon of brown sugar. Into a cereal bowl I added the rhubarb; half an orange, minus peel and pith, and cut into bite-size bits; then, one piece of stem ginger, cubed. Finally, I scattered two-thirds of the cooled oats over the compote, followed by a healthy dollop of Greek yoghurt, a drizzle of honey and the remaining oats.

28th May

On My Mind

Our second date on last year's tour of *The Mousetrap* was Theatre Royal, Northampton. We did nine shows that week. An extra matinee was squeezed in as all eight scheduled performances had been sold out for months. Of course, it rained on our only afternoon off, and I found myself sheltering under the portico of All Saints, the Parish Church. On entering the vestibule I came face to face with a bust of local poet, John Clare. Nearby on the wall was a copy of his poem 'I Am!', written when he was in a mental asylum. Although full of despair and self-pity, there is, in the end, faith in Providence and the restorative power of Nature:

I am: yet what I am none cares or knows,
My friends forsake me like a memory lost;
I am the self-consumer of my woes,
They rise and vanish in oblivious host,

Like shades in love and death's oblivion lost;
And yet I am, and live with shadows tost

Into the nothingness of scorn and noise,
Into the living sea of waking dreams,
Where there is neither sense of life nor joys,
But the vast shipwreck of my life's esteems;
And e'en the dearest – that I loved the best –
Are strange – nay, rather stranger than the rest.

I long for scenes where man has never trod,
A place where woman never smiled or wept;
There to abide with my Creator, God,
And sleep as I in childhood slept:
Untroubling and untroubled where I lie,
The grass below – above the vaulted sky.

(This was today's entry in my anthology.)

I first became aware of John Clare in the seventies, thanks to the celebrated arts programme, *Omnibus*. Freddie Jones played the troubled soul in a heart-breaking biopic-come-drama-documentary. It made a huge impression on me.

This evening mental health is very much on the agenda with a programme focusing on professional footballers and their psychological struggles: *Football, Prince William and Our Mental Health.* For too long, men and boys have been encouraged to keep a stiff upper lip and suppress their feelings.

Depression? Take a walk. Go for a run. Keep busy. Snap out of it. Advice that is well intentioned but inappropriate and misguided.

To admit there is a problem and then share it with a friend is not a sign of weakness. Quite the opposite. It takes a lot of courage to come to that point and then to take the next step and seek professional help. There should be no shame attached. This is an illness, not inadequacy.

Now more than ever, as many endure isolation and loneliness during lockdown, is the time to talk. If you know someone who might be vulnerable, reach out. Time to phone a friend?

29th May

I stray onto controversial political ground this morning. I 'walk' into a famous rose garden. You know the one I mean. This time last week lots of us hadn't heard of a certain adviser. Since then he has become rather *special* to us all. We've seen him up close and we now know what stuff he's made of. He has inspired me to write about him. This is my ode to Dom. I call it:

Smelling of Roses?

(Sing along. I think you know the tune!)
> *I beg your pardon,*
> *Did I hear Sorry in the Rose Garden?*[2]

---

2   A word of explanation. *Dom* is Dominic Cummings who undermined the government guidelines by travelling 260 miles to the North East at the height of the pandemic and by making a further fifty-two-mile round trip to Barnard Castle to 'test his eyesight'. Bowing to political

30th May

Out and About

On my daily walks I'm finding it increasingly difficult to keep two metres away from joggers, cyclists and other walkers, especially on the narrow Thameside path between Brentford and Kew Bridge. There is a notice on a lamp post of the correct etiquette for all users: cyclists to dismount, joggers to be alert, pedestrians to give each other a wide berth. Some follow these instructions, others follow their instincts. I did see some shining examples of social distancing:

A flock of Canada geese, well spaced out;

A family of four – Mum, Dad, a girl and boy, riding their bikes in single file along a cycle lane and not on the pavement;

And lastly, as I was nearly home, half a dozen lads, all under ten years old, boisterous[3] but behaving beautifully.

And I smiled.

Crocodile Smiles – a haiku

Friendly crocodile
passing me in single file;
thanking you, I smile.

---

pressure and unfavourable media coverage, he held a press conference in the rose garden of Number 10 Downing Street on 25th May and 'answered' questions.)

3   I love an explanation that I find of the meaning of the word boisterous: *It's like someone with a spring in her step and a song in her heart, singing to strangers in the street.* Perfect.)

31st May

Friends Remembered (Two Boys: Both Llewellyn)
I've been thinking about Meic and Roger a lot over the last few weeks as the second anniversaries of their deaths have just passed. I knew them for fifty-five and forty-one years respectively.

The extraordinary thing is they shared the same surname, spelled exactly the same way, but they were not related. Swansea was their home town, and they went to the same secondary school – Penlan Multilateral, as it was before it changed into a Comp. Sadly, they died within six weeks of each other. Both of them from cancer.

The two of them were tenors, and sang in choirs. Roger with 'The Orpheus' – Morriston Orpheus Male Voice Choir, while Meic founded one – The Anona Creedy Ensemble – conducted several and sang with many more, not only in Swansea, but Oxford, London and in the Languedoc when he retired to that part of France at the Millennium. They loved acting, too, catching the bug at Swansea Little Theatre in their teens.

Meic was the first boy from Penlan School to win a scholarship to Oxford where he performed and toured with Oxford University Dramatic Society. After graduation he went into teaching, mainly French and Italian, and gained further academic qualifications. But he always found time for extra-mural pursuits, mainly singing and acting.

After a brief spell at Barclays and the Steel Company of Wales, Roger also won a scholarship – not to university but to RADA. He became an accomplished classical actor, notably with the RSC. He enjoyed a successful season at the Stephen Joseph Theatre, Scarborough, for Alan Ayckbourn. But it is for his nuanced and skilful portrayal of Sherlock Holmes, in two solo plays written specifically for him, that he will be best remembered.

The two Llewellyns never got on that well. Probably because they were too alike. They shared similar political views, well to the right of centre, and could be crabby, pompous and dogmatic. But their good qualities far outshone the negative ones. Sound men to have on your side when times were tough. Practical, supportive, helpful and kind.

They last met at supper in my Brentford home five years ago. For some reason an unspoken truce was called, and they really hit it off that night. The conversation flowed as they reminisced about staff and pupils at our alma mater. (Though Penlan could be more accurately described as Alcatraz.) The next day, quite independently, they confessed to me, almost grudgingly, that, contrary to all expectations, they'd had a pleasant evening and enjoyed each other's company. None of us knew then that they would never meet again.

I was caring for Meic in his beautiful home in the Languedoc in April 2018 when I received the news that Roger had died. My instinct was to shield Meic from this as he was nearing the end himself. But an opportunity arose later the same day over a glass of beer, so I passed the information on. Meic was sitting opposite me on a low sofa about eight feet away. With a huge effort he struggled to his feet and shuffled slowly towards me, arms outstretched. We hugged.

"Sorry to hear that, John *bach*. I know you were very

fond of Roger. Of course, I never liked him: he was a very difficult man!"

When I shared this gem with my friend Gareth who knew them both well, he was helpless with laughter:

"You know what, Griffy, that's exactly what Roger would have said if Meic had died first."

True.

Two years on I still miss them both.

Llewellyn And Llewellyn

Two Welsh lads, who were both called Llewellyn,
Left Swansea for London to dwell in.
Meic taught at Sheen School,
But Roger, the fool,
Tried acting, which he did rather well in.

4

JUNE – "MIDSUMMER MADNESS"

Cousins by the Dozen

I have dozens of cousins in USA. This is how it came about…

Doreen Griffiths, my mother's sister, was a G.I. bride. She fell for Steve Voyvodich, an American soldier of Yugoslav heritage. They married and moved to Hazelton, Pennsylvania, and had three children: Danny, Julie and Christine. As a young child I imagined the young Welsh bride sailing away from Southampton on the *Queen Mary*, heading for New York where her darkly handsome beau would be waiting dockside to welcome her. In fact, she left Swansea on a Jamaica-bound banana boat, her bereft parents and siblings waving from the sands, singing: "God be with you till we meet again."

My mother's side of the family weren't the only ones to show this adventurous spirit and go West.

My father's nieces, Jill Francis and her younger sister Dorothy, both fell for Yanks. Jill became a Hardley in

Michigan: Dorothy, a Prairie in Illinois. The 'cousin factory' was soon open for business, and the production line is still going strong, maintained by the succeeding children and grandchildren.

Now, several of these cousins have been badgering me to pass on some of my mother's most popular recipes. I never met anyone who didn't love Aunty Eileen's cakes.

Mam's Meringues & Macaroons

I can't remember what our Eileen did with all the leftover egg yolks when she made these crowd-pleasers, which only required the whites. Her meringues weren't the dry, brittle, sugary concoctions you find with many that are shop-bought, but they were biscuit-coloured and beautifully chewy, as were her macaroons, topped with a halved almond and cooked on rice paper.

I'll let you into some of her secrets…

Meringues

Ingredients

- 2 egg whites
- 4oz/110g caster sugar
- (Preheat the oven to 130°C: Gas Mark a quarter.
  Line two baking trays with baking parchment.)

Method

- Make sure the eggs are at room temperature – at least an hour out of the fridge. Equally important: the bowl you use to whip the egg whites must be free of grease and there must be no yolk in the whites.
- Whisk the egg whites until very stiff. Test by turning the bowl upside down. The mixture should remain motionless. Then, and only then, incorporate the sugar, but you must do this slowly, a little at a time. The classic method is to gradually beat in half the sugar, and then fold in the rest, again in small amounts. If you like a softer meringue, you could use the fold-in method for all the sugar, a teaspoon at a time.
- You can pipe the meringue mixture from a forcing bag, using a large star-shaped nozzle; or simply use two wet dessertspoons.
- Then put into a very cool oven. You don't so much cook them as dry them out. Check after an hour and a half. Should take no longer than two hours. Cool on a wire rack. Sandwich two meringues together with whipped double cream.

3rd June

Lemon Layer

What I found so admirable about my mother's attitude to cooking was she was always open to fresh ideas. She and her cousin Betty were constantly on the lookout for new recipes, and would often set aside a whole day to experiment. I can remember sampling Japanese biscuits, a mixture of meringue and ground hazelnuts, sandwiched together with buttercream and topped with circles of icing; Viennese whirls that melted in the mouth; pineapple tarts that were superior to anything purchased in a cake shop.

Eileen also teamed up with Edith Evans – no, not the '*Handbag*?!' actress, but a friend and fellow foodie who was equally talented in the kitchen. They devoted days to 'cook-ups' as they called them. The results were invariably yummy.

Mam had good old standbys that she would often serve up for dessert. She suffered with poor circulation so her hands were cool enough to turn out thin, crisp, buttery pastry. Apple tart was a great favourite and beyond praise. Her lemon meringue pie was made with condensed milk, topped with heavenly clouds of meringue, which somehow managed to be crisp *and* soft. Sometimes the base was a sponge-cake flan case, which made a nice change from pastry.

A late addition to her repertoire was lemon layer, which was an immediate hit with me. As soon as I'd licked the last spoonful I demanded the recipe. It is now my go-to pud at this time of year, served with strawberries in early to mid-summer, and later on with my preference, raspberries.

"Go on, have some more," I can hear Mam say, "it's only water!"

Lemon Layer

Ingredients

- Zest and juice of an unwaxed lemon
- 1oz/25g caster sugar
- 1 pint/570ml full-fat milk (Sorry, semi-skimmed or see-through milk won't do.)
- 2 large eggs at room temperature (Out of the fridge for at least an hour.)
- 1 pack of lemon jelly, broken into small pieces
- 3 fluid ounces/75ml of double cream ("Excuse me, Eileen: water?")

You will need

- A two-pint pudding basin, lightly coated with sunflower oil; or four highball glasses - no greasing required
- A balloon whisk
- Another two bowls, one for the egg whites: the other for the yolks
- An electric hand whisk

Method

- Separate the yolks from the whites and put into two bowls. Put milk, juice and zest into a saucepan and bring slowly to the boil. Don't be alarmed: it will curdle. Meanwhile add the sugar to the yolks and mix together with a balloon whisk. Pour the milk mixture, just before boiling point is reached, over the yolks stirring vigorously with the whisk, till it looks like custard. Add the jelly that you've already broken into small pieces and beat until dissolved.

- Now, back to the whites. Beat with an electric hand whisk until they form soft peaks. Fold gently into the jelly and custard combo with a metal tablespoon. Don't overwork it. Pour into the pudding basin if you would like to turn it out onto a plate the next day, or into tall glasses, which saves the faff of turning out the 'mousse'. Whichever way you choose, cover with cling film and chill in the fridge overnight.

- You're in for a pleasant surprise.
- By the next day there will be three distinct layers, which will each have a different texture when you tuck in.

Well done, Eileen. Another winner.

4th June

School Dinners

If the last few months have taught us anything it's that we should be prepared for the unexpected. There are very few certainties in life. We see in straight lines: our eyes can't see around corners. The future is unpredictable. Unless, of course, you were Aunty Gertie. She'd often have a go at fortune-telling, and on at least one occasion was spectacularly prescient. One particular forecast concerned my parents, and a complete career change for them both in the summer of 1966.

Up until that point they had never worked together, although before the war they had both been employed by Dr Leslie George, a Swansea GP. Harold, my father, was Dr George's chauffeur and would have had time on his hands when the doctor was holding his twice-daily surgery. That's when the young driver saw his chance of chatting up the young, blond housekeeper, under the guise of helping her with the chores. And that's how he and Eileen got together, after initial resistance on her part; but that's another story for another day.

They married in 1940. I came along seven years later, and my brother seven years after that. When we were growing up in a prefab in Ravenhill, Dad was working as a die-polisher for the Aluminium, Wire and Cable Company in Port Tennant; Eileen meanwhile supplemented the family income by being the 'lady what did' for several middle-class households. As a result of their hard work, by the mid-sixties we had 'never had it so good'. Dad was able to buy his own car at last, and we moved out of a council property into a three-bedroom house, purchased from Harold's brother, Dan. It was so posh that we even had a piano in the parlour…"What about Aunty Gertie?"

Sorry, I digressed…

Auntie Gertie came to tea sometime in the spring of 1966, or it might have been '67; certainly no later than that. She was quite a character, and wasn't really an aunt; in fact no relation at all, just a friend of my mother's. She fancied herself as a bit of a clairvoyant. This particular day, when Mam was about to clear the table, Gertie stopped her:

"Wait a minute, Eileen, I'd like to read your tea leaves."

(This was, of course, 'BB' – before bags – so there were always a few stray sodden leaves in the bottom of every cup.)

Now Eileen wasn't in the least superstitious and didn't hold with fortune-telling, preferring to trust in the will of the Almighty, but there was no point arguing with her psychic friend when her mind was made up. She grabbed Mam's cup, gave it an extravagant swirl, tipped the slops into the saucer and examined what remained, closely…

"Eileen, you're going to have a new job; and it involves children…"

"Nonsense!" protested Eileen. Before Harold could echo this, Gertie snatched *his* cup and saucer, and repeated her practised sequence: swirl, tip, tell:

"Harold, you're not going to believe this, but you're about to have a new job, too; and what's more it's going to be with Eileen. I can see lots of children looking down at you both…"

And that is exactly what happened. In less than six weeks they took up their new posts in Oakleigh House, a prep school in a genteel, well-heeled part of town. (Which is what Swansea was then, not gaining 'city' status until investiture year – 1969.)

The kitchen where Mam prepared the school meals was on the ground floor, and at morning break the children would peer down from the corridor above, trying to see what might be the treat that day, keeping fingers crossed that it might be 'Crispie'.

'Crispie' was possibly the favourite among the desserts that Mrs Francis served up for the privileged staff and children of Oakleigh. In fact, I feel sorry for two famous ex-pupils who never had the 'EE' (emotional experience) of tasting this confection:

Michael Heseltine, the Tory ex-Minister, who was there years before Mam's tenure; and **Alun Wyn-Jones**, the legendary Welsh Rugby captain, who hadn't even been born then. But **Eddie Izzard**, who was there in 1968, must have been one of the lucky ones.

I include the recipe here so you can give it a go for yourself. My brother has made it twice during lockdown. He and his wife, Hazel, are just two among the many in Swansea who love our Eileen's 'Crispie'.

Crispie

Ingredients

- A quarter* of unsalted butter (110g)
- A quarter* of your finest toffee
- A quarter* of pink and white marshmallows
- 6oz Rice Krispies (175g)

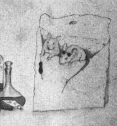

You will need

- A very large saucepan, preferably with a heavy bottom
- A wooden spoon for constant stirring
- A baking tray, roughly 9"x12" (23cm x 30cm)
- And, most importantly a very sweet tooth

Method

- Put the butter, toffee and marshmallows into a saucepan over a low heat. Stir to mix well and to avoid sticking. When all is melted and melded, take off the heat and pour in the Rice Krispies. Turn into the tray, pushing down firmly with the back of a wooden spoon to get an even spread and consistent thickness. Cool. Put into the fridge overnight. Cut into bite-size squares the next day. The bigger your mouth, the bigger the pieces and the greater your 'EE'.

You will need your own teeth, but even these will be under threat. But, hey, it will be worth it. Get stuck in.

*For those born after February 1971, a quarter is 4oz in old money.

5th June

Mrs T's Pikelets

As I've mentioned before, my mother was very complimentary about other people's cooking and baking. The first time she tried Mrs T's pikelets she declared them far superior to her own, in fact the best she'd ever tasted. I don't want to be disloyal, but she was right. They were velvety smooth and very moreish. Unless you had an iron will it was impossible to restrict yourself to just the one.

They are extremely versatile. Try them:

For breakfast with the addition of blueberries in the batter, topped with crisp streaky bacon and maple syrup;

As a tea-time treat served while still warm, with butter – preferably Welsh, which is so salty, it sweats; or experiment with other toppings, for example, unsalted butter, blackcurrant jam and blueberries.

Try substituting them for scones in the classic cream tea.

For years I've made small ones, cutting down the sugar content to a pinch, and serving them with crème fraiche and smoked salmon. A less complicated version of traditional blinis. A wow at finger buffets.

I imagine Mrs T – or Megan, as I was allowed to call her once I hit thirty – would not have approved:

"John *bach*, stop messing about. Serve my pikelets just as they are, hot from the bakestone, and don't stint on the butter."

Before I launch into the recipe, a few words by way of explanation.

A pikelet is what some call a *Scotch pancake*, or others, a *drop-scone*. They were originally Welsh and called *bara*

Mrs T's Tried, Tested and Tasted Recipe for Pikelets

Ingredients

- 8oz/225g self-raising flour
- 1oz/25g caster sugar
- A pinch of salt
- 2 eggs
- 1 teaspoon baking powder
- Half a pint/275ml of full-fat milk

Method:

- For the batter: Sieve the dry ingredients into a bowl. Make a well in the centre and beat in the eggs first, and then gradually whisk in the milk, incorporating a little at a time until you have a smooth batter.

To cook

- Lightly grease the griddle (or substitute), and warm on the hob. You can test if it's hot enough by dropping a teaspoon of the mixture onto the warming surface. The batter should set almost at once, and begin to bubble within one minute. If not, wait a while longer.
- Drop from a tablespoon. Cook for a minute or two until the surface is covered with bubbles. Turn carefully with a palette knife and cook the flipside. Press the top with the knife after a minute. If no liquid oozes out, the pikelet is ready. Lift out and put onto a clean tea towel on a wire cooling rack and cover with the cloth to keep warm and moist.

Ta, Mrs T.

pyglyd, which was later shortened to *pyglyd*. The word spread to the West Midlands where it was anglicised to *picklets*, and eventually *pikelets*.

A bakestone was a traditional Welsh griddle. A non-stick frying pan with a thick bottom will serve just as well.

6th June

Another Day: Another Anniversary

Seventy-six years ago today, 160,000 Allied troops landed on the beaches of Normandy. Operation Overlord began. The largest seaborne invasion in history. It was a huge turning point in the fight against the Nazi menace. An estimated 19,000 soldiers from both sides died on that day: 6th June 1944. Private Harold George Francis, my dad, was one of the fortunate ones, otherwise I wouldn't be writing this piece now; and if he had survived but the war had not been won, probably not in English. We owe an enormous debt to those who made the ultimate sacrifice and also to their compatriots who survived.

We will remember them. The poem for today – 'Song of the Dying Gunner' – is by the brilliant Cornish writer Charles Causley. The line about the GWR struck a chord. I thought of my dad's train journeys home during the war when he was granted the rare privilege of compassionate leave. The first, in October 1940, was a happy occasion: forty-eight hours so he could marry his sweetheart, Eileen Griffiths. A few months later, in February 1941, he returned home in more sombre mood and witnessed at first hand the destruction of his town after three nights of sustained bombing by the Luftwaffe. He was met by an uncle who acted as his guide to Manselton, as so many landmarks had been flattened that Harold would have struggled on his own to find his way through the rubble in the blackout. A happy reunion came late in 1945 when the newly demobbed private boarded the train in Paddington, arriving four hours later at High Street Station, where his loved ones were waiting on the platform, tearful and open-armed.

7th June

Giovanni's Cherry Tree

The starlings are back. Each year around this time they descend on my neighbour's cherry tree and indulge in a feeding frenzy. Giovanni indulges them, content for them to strip the upper branches, which are beyond his reach even on a ladder. He's not greedy. Enough of the crop remains on the middle and lower boughs for him and his family. There must be over a hundred birds, constantly moving so that the image of the tree pixelates, creating a mirage in the morning sun. I reach for my tablet and start videoing this phenomenon, and almost immediately they all stop gorging themselves and fly off. Something disturbed them. I don't think it was me. And it certainly wasn't the kindly Giovanni. He'll be harvesting tomorrow when his avian friends have had their fill.

8th June

Friends, Fruit and Flowers

After breakfast this morning I paid my daily visit to the

garden to see how things were faring after the welcome rain of the last few days. The beans, of course, will still need watering. As my ex-neighbour Ela used to say: "A bucket of water on your beans, come rain or shine." She was right, they are thirsty plants. I'm encouraged to see they have started to flower. I check up on the hostas too. Have the slugs and snails taken advantage of the wet weather and started to perforate my much-prized plants? I'm relieved to find that so far they seem to have escaped.

Later I decide on the shortest of walks as the weather has turned a bit dodgy. I can only have been away for a quarter of an hour. When I return I find that two friends have left gifts of fruit. In the lean-to in the front garden where the recycling bins are housed are two ripe and fragrant mangoes; and hanging on the back-garden gate is a carrier bag full of cherries from Giovanni's tree. His generosity is not confined to the birds.

One mango will make an exotic breakfast tomorrow with granola and yoghurt; the other will be divided in half, one half to be chunked, the other liquidised to make a coulis, and then combined with ice cream to make a refreshing dessert.

Then I turned my attention to the cherries. After washing them I put the ripest to one side to sample later. For the rest, I decided not to stone them but made a tiny slit in each with a small sharp knife. I put them into a saucepan and covered them with three dessertspoons of caster and one tablespoon each of kirsch, white wine and water. The alcohol is not essential but the kirsch gives a heady flavour to the resulting poached fruit. I cooked them for about twenty minutes on a low heat. While they were cooling I sterilised a Kilner jar ready for these ruby beauties. Before I decant these I try the uncooked ones. *Yes, of course, I counted the stones:*"Tinker, tailor, soldier, sailor…"

I'm *a beggar man.* At least I'm not *a thief.* To tell the truth, it was *beggar man* the *second time around.* That's sixteen cherries in all. Greedy Griffs!

Two of my indoor plants have been giving me enormous pleasure during quarantine, and not just because of their intrinsic beauty, but because they both came from friends, which means a lot. A blousy, pink African violet was grown from a cutting by my green-fingered friend, Holly, and my stephanotis was a flat-warming present eight years ago from another chum, Jeff. Both are gifts that keep on giving.

Perhaps one of the best gifts that friends can give us, now more than ever, is *Time.*

A precious gift indeed.

9th June

In Praise of the Tomato, the Blushing Belladonna

"There's ripe tommy-toes for the gentry, And bloaters for the likes of you…"

The opening of Jerry's song in *Lark Rise to Candleford.* I played the part in a production at Cheltenham's Everyman Theatre in 1986. One day the arrival of Jerry's cart in the hamlet causes quite a stir as there is a surprising new item among the usual fish, fruit and veg. Laura, the heroine, is intrigued by a basket of red and yellow fruit:

"What are those?" she asked old Jerry.

"Love-apples, me dear. Love-apples, they be; though some hignorant folks be a callin' 'em tommy-toes. But you don't want any o' they – nasty, sour things they be, as only gentry can eat. You have a nice sweet orange wi' your penny."

But Laura felt she must taste the love-apples and insisted upon having one.

"Don't 'ee go tryin' to eat it now," one woman urged. "It'll only make 'ee sick. I know because I had one of the nasty horrid things at our Minnie's."

And nasty, horrid things tomatoes remained in the popular estimation for years; though most people today would prefer them to the watery insipidity of our larger, smoother tomato.

This comment from the author, Flora Thompson, holds true for most of the Dutch and Spanish tomatoes we import in huge numbers, especially in the winter months. An abomination. What a difference when you eat domestically produced ones in season. Better still, grow your own if you have the room. I'm growing some in pots this year. The ones that ripen I will eat in salads or use in cooking. But I will be very happy if most of them stay green as then I can use them to make Chapel Chutney.

But more of that another day.

9th June

All Greek to Me
This morning I ventured on my longest excursion since

lockdown started. I had to get a solicitor to witness some probate papers on Meic's estate. He died in France two years ago and I'm one of his executors. That's not a job I would wish on my worst enemy, let alone a friend. Dealing with the French authorities is proving tricky, time-consuming and very frustrating. I won't go on.

Anyway, the nearest solicitor brave enough to risk a meeting face to face – or should that be mask to mask? – is based in Barnes Village, over five miles from home. Too far to walk. And I don't drive. Can't risk an Uber. Nothing for it but to don my industrial mask that makes me look like Hannibal Lecter, and get a train from Brentford to Barnes. But I was still worried. However, my fears proved unfounded as the train was practically empty. Getting off the train I decide to walk the mile from the station to Barnes Village. As well as the mask, I was wearing a jacket as I'm an old-fashioned cove who always dresses smartly for business meetings. My one concession to the hot weather is that I dispense with a tie. By the time I reach the end of Rocks Lane I'm hot under that loosened collar and have a face like a ruddy, ripe beef tomato.

Which brings me to the point of this rambling…

While I'm engaged on matters legal, my sainted neighbour Mary is out shopping, and has promised to get me some tomatoes as I fancy a BLT for tomorrow's lunch. Mary is half-Greek, half-Scottish and is at home in both cuisines. And she's an outstanding cook. A tomato is a favourite ingredient with her. It shines in soup with orzo, it graces her very Greek chicken casserole, flavoured with oregano and cinnamon, but it is firmly centre stage, the star attraction in her recipe for:

Stuffed Tomatoes

Ingredients

- 6 large beef tomatoes
- 4 fluid oz / 125ml passata
- 2 medium onions, finely diced
- 2 garlic cloves, crushed
- 2oz / 50g minced beef/lamb
- Half a teaspoon tomato puree
- Generous pinch of sugar
- 2oz / 50g arborio rice
- One and a half tablespoons parsley, chopped
- 1 teaspoon each of dill and oregano
- Salt and pepper
- (Preheat oven to Gas Mark 3; 160°C Fan)

Method

- Cut lids off the tomatoes and scoop out the flesh with a small sharp spoon. Put the pulp in a blender and pulse to a thick juice with the passata, sugar, salt and pepper.
- Heat olive oil in a medium-sized pan and sauté the onions over a low heat until translucent, adding the garlic after a few minutes. Now put in the mince and brown for five minutes. Add most of the tomato sauce and bring to the boil. Stir in the rice and simmer for 7-8 minutes. Remove from the heat and add the herbs. Sprinkle the cavity in each tomato with a little salt. Fill each tomato with the rice mixture and put the lids back on. Arrange tomatoes in an ovenproof dish and pour in the rest of the tomato sauce and a dash of olive oil.

Bake for an hour and test with a skewer
to see if they are done. They might
need a little longer.

- If you don't eat meat you can omit
it and double the amount of rice.
A few pine kernels, raisins, chopped
olives or capers could be added, but not
all of them: just one extra ingredient as the tomato is the star after
all.

10th June

Better than Heinz

As today is unseasonably chilly my thoughts turn to soup; and tomato soup in particular. I must confess that when time is short, when I'm very busy – and when no one's looking – I have been known to open a tin of the Heinz variety. No such excuse at the moment as I have time on my hands. Speaking for myself, that is. I know lots of parents are having to work from home, do all the household chores, feed the family and turn the kitchen into a classroom. From my experience of teaching youngsters I know almost all of them love cooking and can become highly skilled at it, so I'm sure lots of kids are having a go during lockdown. It's a great life skill to have. You'll never starve and you'll make many friends.

Today's recipe was given to me by Angela in Little Missenden, though it originates in South Africa – the Kwande Kitchen, to be precise. From the first mouthful I was smitten, refusing to leave the table until she'd promised to give me the recipe. It was the texture as much as the taste that appealed, and I was to learn that both were achieved by the seemingly extravagant amount of olive oil used: 100ml. A lot, I know, but don't stint.

Spoil yourself: you deserve it.

Angela's Tomato Soup

Ingredients

- 2 medium onions
- 1 stick of celery + 1 carrot
- 3 cloves garlic (all four of these ingredients finely diced)
- 3.5 fl oz / 100 ml olive oil
- Two-pint jug full of chopped fresh tomatoes (or 400g if using tinned)

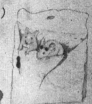

- 3 tablespoons tomato puree
- 1 glass white wine – I leave the size to you!
- 2 sprigs of fresh thyme, or a good pinch of dried
- 35 fl oz / 1 litre stock (chicken or vegetable)
- Salt and pepper
- Pinch of caster sugar

Method

- Warm the oil in a saucepan over a low heat. Add the diced onion, carrot and celery and sweat for a good 10 minutes until they have all started to soften and the onion is just beginning to colour. Put in the garlic and cook for 2 minutes, stirring to combine the aromatics. Then in go the wine, tomatoes and puree. Simmer for 5 minutes before adding the stock, thyme leaves and seasoning. Simmer gently for 30 minutes. Cool for 5 minutes before blending. For extra smoothness, pass through a sieve. Don't be tempted to add cream when serving as the soup is rich enough with all that oil. Perhaps a sprig of basil and a few croutons? Just the thing for a cold, drizzly day in June.

Gazpacho can wait until the summer returns...

11th June

Chapel Chutney

Vera Batty was my first Sunday school teacher. I was probably three years old when I started in her class. It was quite an adventure, as to get to her schoolroom you had to leave the Gospel Hall by the back door and climb a flight of quarry-tiled steps to the small outbuilding. I remember it was overwhelmingly hot in summer but rather nippy in winter as the only means of heating was an old-fashioned, coal-burning, cast-iron stove in the centre of the room. We sat around it in a tight, happy-clappy circle, chorusing favourites like 'Climb, Climb up Sunshine Mountain' – with our eager faces all aglow. We trumpeted with Joshua and brought Jericho's walls tumbling down; we drank at the brook with Gideon; we fired stones from our slings at Goliath; marched up the ramp of Noah's Ark with the animals, two by two; and we dared to be a Daniel in the lion's den. And as we sang the songs of Zion we acted out the stories with suitable actions, gestures and facial contortions. We loved climbing into the Sycamore tree with Zaccheus and would be reduced to helpless laughter when "the foolish man", ignoring all advice, built his house "upon the sand". "When the rains came down and the floods came up, the house on the sand went, 'Splat!'"

Vera would also encourage us to come up with imaginative suggestions as to how we thought Moses was able to cross the Red Sea, before supplying us with the orthodox Exodus account of events. How we enjoyed joining in as Jehovah blew with a mighty wind. We *puff-puff-puffed* until almost hyperventilating, but the path through the Red Sea was made and the Israelites miraculously escaped.

It was in Vera's class that I learned to read and to train my memory as we had to learn a verse of scripture each week. And draw pictures and eventually write our own versions of these gripping stories when we were a little older. Then, before you could say "Nebuchadnezzar", it was time to leave Vera's class and go up, or *down* in this case, to an intermediate class where we began to study for the annual scripture exam. Every year, too, there was prize-giving: a book, signed by the superintendent, and awarded for 'Good Attendance'.

But I never forgot Vera and the good start she gave me. I can see her now, smiling and welcoming, in her warm, Welsh, all-weathers, brown woollen coat and matching hat; and still hear her unfailing greeting:

"Hello, lovely boy. How are you?"But I have a tangible memory too. Vera Batty's mother's recipe for green tomato chutney. Every autumn without fail I would be the grateful recipient of a jar of this glorious creation: spicy, sharp and sweet. Eventually Vera gave me the recipe, written by her own fair hand. A golden treasure indeed. I have christened it:

Chapel Chutney

Ingredients

- 2lb / 900g green tomatoes
- 2lb / 900g onions
- 2lb / 900g Bramley apples
- 2lb / 900g granulated or preserving sugar
- 1 pint / 570ml malt vinegar
- good pinch salt
- 3 teaspoons turmeric
- 1 teaspoon each of: chilli powder, ground ginger and ground cloves
- 2 tablespoons mustard seeds

Method

- First, wash and dice the tomatoes. Not too finely; you want a bit of texture. It's chutney, not sauce. Pieces should be just larger than a thumbnail. Put into a large preserving pan and add the salt, sugar and pour in the vinegar. Then get ready for tears as you tackle the onions. I find it does help to wear glasses, keep rinsing your hands and whistle while you work. Try soaking them in cold water beforehand; it makes them easier to peel. Cut them into quarters. Zap them in a food processor for 5-10 seconds. You want them to be chopped not pulped. Do a small batch at a time. Put them into the pan. Finally, the apples. Wash, peel, core and dice. So that's everything in the pot except for the spices. Their turn will come.
- Give the mixture a good stir with a long-handled wooden spoon, and bring to the boil. Keep lightly boiling for 45 minutes, stirring now and then. Sieve in the turmeric and mix well. Boil for another 10 minutes.

Then introduce the ginger, chilli and cloves. Stir in well again to get even distribution and no lumps. Cook for a further 5 minutes. By this time you should have achieved a jam-like consistency. If not set thick enough, boil a little longer, stirring constantly to avoid sticking. Take off the heat and stir in the mustard seeds. Cover with a clean, damp tea towel and rest for 12 hours. The chutney, that is, not you. Though you might be excused for feeling jaded after all that chopping, mincing and stirring.

- The next day sterilise the jars and dry in a low oven for 10 minutes or so. Half a dozen jars should suffice, depending on the size. Bottle, label, put a circle of greaseproof paper on the top of each and seal. The joy of this chutney is that you don't have to wait months for it to mature. You can tuck in the next day. But it will keep in a cool dark place for a year. Somehow I don't think it will hang around that long.

12th June

The Last of the Tomatoes

A silly thing to say because mine haven't even started to flower yet. What I mean is, my last post on the subject of tomatoes. Time for a change tomorrow.

Even though the summer has deserted us for the moment, I'm sure it will return, and when it does I shall be looking up two of my old continental friends, Gazpacho and Tricolore.

Before I introduce them, let's hear it for the virtue of a simple tomato sandwich. Freshly made, just as it is, with salt and pepper, or with the addition of basil; a basic cheese and tomato filling, or as a toastie; as the sweet, juicy element in a classic BLT; and a particular favourite of mine, alternate slices of tomato and hard-boiled egg between two pieces of bread, liberally spread with mayonnaise.

Tricolore

A great summer stand-by, and perhaps the most colourful of starters.
It's named after the Italian flag. I think it well worth investing in buffalo
mozzarella. You'll pay a bit more, but you don't need that much. Avos are
plentiful and affordable, and if teamed with your own
home-grown tomatoes and basil, you'll be quids in.

You will need (for four)

- 8oz / 225g mozzarella
- 2 medium/large avocados
- 1lb / 450g tomatoes
- Two dozen basil leaves
- Salt and pepper
- Squeeze of lemon

The dressing

- 1 small clove of garlic, crushed
- Teaspoon salt
- Pinch sugar
- A few twists of black pepper
- Half teaspoon tomato puree
- Teaspoon Dijon mustard (French, I know!)
- 1 tablespoon vinegar
- 5 tablespoons olive oil

Method

- Make sure the tomatoes and avos have never been in the fridge. The mozzarella is another matter. It's a lot easier to slice if it comes straight out of the fridge. Cut into twelve slices and put three on each plate. Do the same with the tomatoes, though you'll probably end up with more slices, depending on their size.

Lastly, the avocado. Slices or bite-sized chunks complete the stripes of the 'flag'. You can squeeze a little lemon juice over the avo at this point before pouring the dressing over all and covering with clingfilm for 10 minutes before 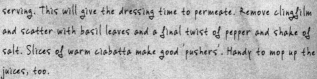 serving. This will give the dressing time to permeate. Remove clingfilm and scatter with basil leaves and a final twist of pepper and shake of salt. Slices of warm ciabatta make good 'pushers'. Handy to mop up the juices, too.

Gazpacho
(Again for four – a nice square number)

Ingredients

- 5oz / 150g tomatoes, chopped
- 1 green pepper, de-seeded and cut into quarters
- 6 spring onions, washed and hairy fringe removed
- Half a large cucumber, peeled
- 2 cloves of garlic
- Heaped tablespoon of washed coriander, leaves only
- 1 dessertspoon tomato puree
- Half a pint / 275ml tomato juice, chilled
- 2 fluid oz / 55ml olive oil
- 1 tablespoon sherry vinegar
- Quarter pint / 150ml ice-cold water

Method

- Before liquidising the first six ingredients, reserve one tomato, one spring onion, a small piece of pepper and an inch of the cucumber. Chop these into tiny dice to be passed round at the table. Can also make a few small croutons if liked, or even a hard-boiled egg, coarsely grated. Blend the remaining tomatoes (skinned), pepper, onions and cucumber with the garlic until liquid in a processor or blender. Strain into a clean jug or bowl through a sieve and press vigorously with a wooden spoon to extract all the juice. Discard the pulp that's left.
- Pour the liquid back into the food-processor or liquidiser, then add the tomato puree, half a pint of tomato juice and the coriander leaves and pulse for twenty seconds. With the motor running add the oil in a

steady trickle until well-combined (about a further thirty seconds). Pour the soup into a large bowl with the vinegar and iced water, and mix well with a balloon whisk. Taste at this point and season with salt and pepper. Cover and refrigerate for at least two hours. Serve in bowls you've pre-chilled in the freezer, and pass round the accompaniments.

- Perfect way to start an al fresco lunch on a summer's day. When summer returns, that is. Fingers crossed.

13th June

Friends Reunited

I'm slowly working my way through the psalms: one for each day of *my splendid isolation*. (Is irony still in order? I do hope so.)

Psalm 83 today. The next book in the Old Testament is *Proverbs.* But it's not just the Bible that is 'full of wise saws and modern instances': the whole of world literature is littered with them, and every society has its own pithy epigrams that are passed on to each succeeding generation.

I've been thinking of friends a lot during this time of separation, and thinking what I miss most about them. And how I'll not take them for granted, and will value them more in the future. As Shakespeare put it: "Keep thy friend under thy own life's key."

Thankfully, restrictions are gradually being relaxed. This evening I'm about to walk three miles to a friend in Chiswick to have a natter over drinks and snacks, at a safe distance, of course. I'm reminded of the old saying, immortalised on many a Victorian cross-stitch sampler:

"The Road to the House of a Friend is never long."

(Some versions say *Door* instead; I prefer *House*: we've been kept waiting outside long enough.)

I'd like to recommend a poem on this theme to you: 'The Pleasures of Friendship' by Stevie Smith. Heart-warming.

There is so much to look forward to over the next week. Tomorrow a Zoom quiz for six at six; morning coffee and cheese scones with two chums on Tuesday; and, at last, a walk in the recently reopened Kew Gardens mid-week.

Small steps, but we're starting to connect once more.

(At the end of this post I asked for suggestions for a new proverb for these dark days. The challenge was to complete the following:

"A day without a friend is like…?"

The prize? Tea at Mafeking Mansions once this lousy plague is over. There are some splendid submissions. A few are food/drink-related:

A day without a friend is like…
bacon without laverbread; fish without chips; gin without tonic.

Some are on a nature theme. A day without a friend is like…

a lawn without daisies; a skylark with no song.

My American cousin Danny, who's a man of the cloth, offers:

… like a day without God's Grace.

And I love: *… like a candle without a flame.*

The most poignant – and personal – is: *… like a stage without an actor.*

15th June

Today marks a grim anniversary.

Grenfell's Heart

Thirty-six months.
Seventy-two peals
tolling for the dead.
Then, from a different tongue,
a litany of names.
Behind each name a life lost,
mourned and missed:
a life that mattered.
Grenfell's heart,
green with hope,
bleeds red.

16th June

Bloomsday

The action in James Joyce's masterpiece, *Ulysses*, is crammed into one day, 16th June. The hero, Leopold Bloom, gives his name to today's commemoration. In my daily anthology I find the poem, '*Ecce Puer*' – 'Behold the Boy', which I'd like to share. I must confess I never knew that Joyce wrote so much poetry. After early efforts in this field he gave it up, thinking it over-sentimental, and opted for a grittier and more public form in his prose works. It was as if he progressed from composing chamber music to grand opera. *The Dubliners, Finnegan's Wake* and *Ulysses* all show a heightened poetic style. The latter, a work on a truly epic scale.

What a contrast to the tender song below, private and personal. It marks the conjunction of life and death: the birth of Joyce's grandson and the death of his own father; and it ends with a *cri de coeur*. He didn't return to his father's death-bed in Ireland. Guilt-ridden, he begs for forgiveness. From its title to the closing lines there are echoes of the scriptures, and it is full of biblical imagery and language. Indeed, the title recalls Pilate's *Ecce Homo*; the second line replicates Isaiah's prophesy of the Messiah: the ending a re-imagining of Christ's words from the cross:

Ecce Puer

> *Of the dark past*
> *A child is born.*
> *With joy and grief*
> *My heart is torn.*
> *Calm in his cradle*
> *The living lies.*
> *May love and mercy*
> *Unclose his eyes!*
> *Young life is breathed*
> *On the glass;*
> *The world that was not*
> *Comes to pass.*
> *A child is sleeping:*

An old man gone.
O, father forsaken,
Forgive your son.

A towering man of letters, who wrote like an angel, must surely by now have been granted a posthumous, paternal pardon.

Amen to that.

17th June

Hiraeth

Yesterday I felt very Irish. Having made the acquaintance of '*Ecce Puer*' in my morning reading I come across an old friend in the evening:

The Lake Isle of Innisfree
by W.B. Yeats

I will arise and go now, and go to Innisfree,
And a small cabin build there, of clay and wattles made:
Nine bean-rows will I have there, a hive for the honey-bee,
And live alone in the bee-loud glade.

And I shall have some peace there, for peace comes
    dropping slow,
Dropping from the veils of the morning to where the
    cricket sings;
There midnight's all a glimmer, and noon a purple glow,
And evening full of the linnet's wings.

I will arise and go now, for always night and day
I hear lake water lapping with sounds by the shore;
While I stand on the roadway, or on the pavements grey,
I hear it in the deep heart's core.

I dedicate this to all my Irish friends, past and present; and to the following in particular: Bob, who is shielding in Mumbles; Tony in West Cross, who writes some fine poems of his own; Barbara in Cheshire, who was for many years the smiling face of Aer Lingus; David in Southall, late of Longford, a great neighbour and generous friend; Angela and Seamus, whom I knew years ago in Hanwell, but with whom I lost touch; and to anyone who currently lives in Butlers Town, Waterford with the surname Walsh – we're probably related.

I'm sure I'm not alone in having experienced similar feelings during lockdown to those expressed by Yeats in his poem: a strong urge to return to a familiar and favourite spot, especially our birthplace. We Welsh have a word for it: *hiraeth*; the Cornish, *hireth*; the Bretons, *hiraezh*. These pangs of homesickness are not confined to the Celts, but are universal and find expression in songs and poems:

'Home-Thoughts from Abroad' and 'The Soldier' are two fine English examples.

And who could fail to be moved by Kenneth McKellar singing:

I am far beyond the sea, but my heart will ever be
At home in dear old Scotland wi' my ain folk…

Or the Irish tenor, John McCormack, promising:

I'll take you home again Kathleen
Across the ocean wild and wide...

The Psalmist captured it perfectly:

By the rivers of Babylon
There we sat down,
Yea, we wept,
When we remembered Zion."

(Immortalised in the Boney M version.)

Personally, I'm missing dear old Swansea:

And she'll be waiting there for me, she'll be glad to see me;
And I'll never leave my town again: a fortune won't persuade
me...

Oh, yes I'm missing them all, the Swansea Jacks – and Jills. And not just the people, but the place: its open skies and golden sands, the limestone cliffs and even the soft, salty rain. But, most of all, post-pandemic, I'm looking forward to cockles and laverbread from Swansea's award-winning market, and, inevitably, an ice cream from Joe's up town or down the Mumbles. Tidy, mun.

18th June

The Forces' Sweetheart
Dame Vera Lynn died today surrounded by her nearest and dearest. The statement read:

The family are deeply saddened to announce the passing of one of Britain's best-loved entertainers at the age of 103.

And so say all of us. I feel a letter coming on…

Dear Vera,
You won all our hearts. And we'll never meet your like again.
Sincerely yours,
A grieving, grateful country. x

R.I.P.

19th June

The Dreamers of Dreams

This year we have had three deaths in Mafeking Avenue. One was from cancer and came well before Covid-19 took hold. As far as I know, the other two weren't Corona-related either.

But amongst the sadness and loss, there has been good news too.

Our street, always warm and welcoming, has become even more friendly during lockdown. Clapping for the NHS and other key workers every Thursday for ten weeks has been a great ice-breaker. A nodding acquaintance has become a chatty chum; a familiar face now has a name. To those I already knew well, Irene, Mary, David, Peter, Tommy and Pip, I can now add Genevieve, Sam, Fiona, Toyah, Yvonne,

Joseph and the newest of newcomers, ten-week-old Elijah. His mum would often bring him out to witness the weekly tribute. Unperturbed, he usually slept on during the loud, prolonged applause.

There are some great names in that list of neighbours. I'd like to concentrate on two of them: Elijah and Joseph.

The story of Joseph I feel sure is familiar to most people from RE lessons, Sunday School or, most likely these days, from the Rice/Lloyd Webber Musical, *Joseph and the Amazing Technicolor Dreamcoat*… and yes, I have, and no, I played his dad, Jacob. I also directed it with a group of talented ten- and eleven-year-olds in a primary school near Wormwood Scrubs, but that's another story. Back to the biblical version…

It is obvious to Joseph's brothers that he is their father's favourite son. A suspicion confirmed, as far as his siblings are concerned, by the gift of a multicoloured coat to Joseph by the doting Jacob. They are already fed up with Joseph's frequent, unsolicited repetition and interpretations of his dreams. The coat clinches it: Joseph has to go. They sell him into slavery, daub his precious coat in the blood of a goat and present the splattered garment to Jacob as proof that their brother has been killed by a wild animal…

Spoiler Alert
This is not an end but a beginning for the outcast. Joseph prospers in Egypt, first as a steward in Potiphar's house, and eventually, after false accusations and wrongful imprisonment, as prime minister in Pharaoh's court. All because of his ability to interpret dreams and then to cleverly avoid the dire forecasts

by identifying what must be done and providing ingenious solutions.

Every generation needs men and women of such vision and integrity. Idealism coupled with practical skill.

And then, much later in the Old Testament, we discover the prophet Elijah. He was an outspoken man of God, who was not afraid to speak truth unto power. And an evil power it was: King Ahab and his Consort, Jezebel. Although there is a price on his head, Elijah confronts these unscrupulous and dangerous enemies head on. This is another gripping read. Eventually, Elijah triumphs over tyranny, passing on his mantle to his disciple, Elisha. The struggle must go on. His work on earth done, a chariot of fire transports him to his heavenly reward.

That image inspired Blake to pen 'Jerusalem' and Parry to set it to music; gave the makers of *Chariots of Fire* a memorable title; and its powerful imagery was not lost on the freed slave, Wallace Willis, the writer of 'Swing Low, Sweet Chariot', which has been much in the news over recent days. I'm keeping well out of that controversy.

When I ever hear the word 'Elijah' I automatically think of Mendelssohn's oratorio of that name. There are huge set pieces of epic, symphonic and operatic proportions. In other places, the composer uses a "still, small voice" to great effect.

Whatever faith you have, or if you have none, take some time to listen to a pair of examples in this vein: the chorus, 'Lift Thine Eyes' and the chorale, 'Cast Thy Burden upon the Lord'.

Two perfect choices for our times. Pleasing to the ear and gladdening to the spirit.

20th June

He strode the narrow world
Like a Colossus, and we petty men
Walked under his huge legs and peeped about.

Today we mourn the loss of Ian Holm, one of the most talented and versatile actors of his generation, equally at home on stage or screen. His early work in theatre ranged from *Henry V* for the RSC to *The Homecoming* in the West End. Harold Pinter rated him highly, saying: "He puts on a shoe, and it fits."

Millions of movie-goers knew him from *Lord of the Rings*, *Alien* and *Chariots of Fire*. Fewer would have caught his *King Lear*. At 5'5" he must have been the shortest actor ever to have played the "foolish, fond old man". I remember when Richard Eyre, the outgoing Artistic Director, announced on a TV chat show that his swansong at the National Theatre would be *King Lear*, and that Ian Holm would take the title role. I thought he was mad or had misspoken. Perhaps the likeliest explanation was that I had misheard. Surely Ian would play the Fool; ideal casting? But the stricken king? Come off it, Mr Eyre, you cannot be serious. But he was. And how wrong was I.

Ian Holm gave a towering performance. *Every inch a King.*

21st June

Father's Day (or should that be **Fathers' Day?**)
I think I'll plump for the latter as my own father died nearly

fifty years ago. But I think of Harold George Francis today and reread a piece I wrote about him a few years back – *The Visitor* – which formed part of my one-man show, *Chapel, Chums and Chips*. His greatest quality was his sense of humour and I hope some of that has rubbed off.

My Irish friend Tony wrote a moving poem, 'The Glove', about his da and shared it with me. I look it out today and peruse it again:

The Glove

A home visit, the first for a while;
poking around, looking for rods and tackle
to cast, or spin a line.

It must have lain there a year, or more,
dust-covered, bench-webbed;
an age since I saw it worn.

A cast, a last grip;
lighter than expected as I slip it on,
my hand lost in his.

A child again, by wood and river,
his trying to teach,
to reach.

Now no smell, no glove
just the memory of the hand
that never cuffed.

I find a new one as well, 'Father's Hands' by Paul Cookson, and give it the once-over, and am instantly impressed. It's well worth a look.

Later, on my walk, in a quiet corner of St Paul's Park, I recite Dylan Thomas' defiant, 'Do Not Go Gentle', written on the death of his own father, and spare a thought for those who have lost their dads recently, and inwardly with them, I "rage against the dying of the light".

23rd June

Rubies and Diamonds
Anniversaries are coming thick and fast at the moment. Perhaps some of them have passed me by in previous, busier years, unnoticed and unmarked. Now, with more time to stand and stare, there's little excuse to ignore them. Two friends of mine have confided in me recently about significant days they almost missed. My friend Susie totally forgot it was her son Truan's birthday and hastily had to postpone a get-together she'd planned with other friends to spare her embarrassment and his hurt. Then Beryl rang earlier to thank me for the bottle of bubbles I'd given her and Anthony at the weekend. They plan on popping the cork tonight as they've only just realised that this is their Ruby Wedding Anniversary! Luckily the champagne is the right colour for the occasion.

Yesterday marked the anniversary of Queen Victoria's accession to the throne in 1837. Sixty years later she became the longest reigning monarch of these isles – an achievement surpassed by her great-great-granddaughter, Queen Elizabeth II, in 2015. I am now such an old chap that I recall not only each of Her Majesty's Jubilees – Silver, Golden and Diamond – but also her Coronation. It was wet. Our street party on the prefab estate had to be held in various of the neighbours' garages, but we didn't let a drop of rain spoil the celebration; just like the thousands lining the streets of London. Little did we know when we sang, "long to reign over us", in those early June days that our prayers would be answered to such an extent. God *has* saved her, and she has indeed been a *gracious queen*.

Her recent broadcasts have further enhanced her reputation, gained universal respect and endeared her to her people even more. "Here's a health unto Her Majesty!"

Footnote

Clang! I have met several members of the Royal family over the years. Indeed, Prince Edward and I shared the same employer once: Andrew Lloyd Webber. But I've never met the Queen. I felt compelled to write to Her Majesty this spring to wish her a happy birthday and to thank her for her recent uplifting addresses to the nation. I send my letter to Windsor Castle and smile wryly when I realise it has a Slough postcode.

A few weeks later I get a reply. It's in a top-quality cream envelope that bears the monogram 'EIIR' and is postmarked 'WINDSOR CASTLE'. I notice it's franked 'POSTAGE PAID' but not stamped. Perhaps they'd run out of the little perforated squares bearing the Queen's portrait. The paper inside is equally impressive and is headed by the Royal Coat of Arms; the Lion and the Unicorn flanking the heraldic shield. Below them, the motto: 'DIEU ET MON DROIT'.

WINDSOR CASTLE
28ᵗʰ May 2020

Dear Mr Griffiths
The Queen wishes to thank you for the kind message you sent for Easter and her ninety-fourth birthday, and your kind comments about Her Majesty's recent broadcast to the Nation and the Commonwealth.

The Queen much appreciates your thought for her at this time, and hopes that you are keeping safe and well during the current situation.

I am to thank you very much once again for your letter and continuing loyalty and support for Her Majesty.

Yours sincerely…

(And then it's signed by a lady-in-waiting. I can't decipher the hand.) I'm so glad I took the trouble to write.

24th June

Ember Day

That's what it says in my diary today. And again for Friday and Saturday this week. I google it. Ember days happen four times at different seasons of the year and entail three non-consecutive days of abstinence. Not surprised I hadn't heard of them with my Chapel upbringing, as they are marked in the Catholic Church. They are set aside for fasting and prayer; but they have a practical side to them, too. The underlying purpose is for believers to thank the Almighty for the gifts of nature, to learn to be responsible custodians of the environment, and to care for the needy in society. Three laudable aims which are going to be all the more urgent as we emerge from the Covid-19 pandemic.

I have been so grateful to have had an outdoor patch of green to tend during lockdown. My garden has become a refuge. A place for planting, nurturing, growing and relaxing. A godsend really. Many people have not been so fortunate. But at least London, thanks to the Georgians and Victorians, has lots of parks, squares, commons and gardens. A green city. Today I had my first trip to Kew Gardens since they reopened after lockdown. One hundred days without visiting one of my favourite haunts, which is only a twenty-minute walk away. How lucky I am to have this World Heritage site practically on my doorstep. And how the world needs this facility, as in their vaults and laboratories they store the largest mycological collection on the planet, and have seeds, many of endangered species, from all over the world. An institution to treasure.

Two summers ago I was delighted to be cast in a production of Bernstein's *Candide*. This formed part of the Iford Festival that year. Each night we fought back tears as we united in the heartfelt finale, with its vision of a good life, achieved through the simple things, by caring for nature and for each other. Take a few moments to listen to this powerful anthem. I guarantee you will be touched deeply. Its message seems more potent now than ever.

25th June

Care Bear

Surprising how the best ideas come at unexpected times and in the unlikeliest of places. A light-bulb moment might strike when you're lying in the bath. However excited you might be, springing up, shouting, "Eureka!" is not highly recommended.

Today is the anniversary of the founding of the Royal Society for the Prevention of Cruelty to Animals in 1824, after a meeting in a London coffee house. It was granted the Royal Warrant sixteen years later. Although the Victorians felt sentimental about animals, they often treated them inappropriately, and cruelty towards them persisted. We still see vestiges of that today. From time to time there are reports in the media of unspeakable treatment of domestic pets and wildlife. Sadly, refuges are still full of unwanted and abused creatures.

The poem for today is related to this theme and is by the accomplished Cornish poet, Charles Causley: 'My Mother Saw a Dancing Bear'. The captured beast is forced to perform. Its sad eyes seem to be full of longing for the distant forests and the snow, its natural habitat.

We all need to think more about animals and less about ourselves; to care just that bit more, especially today as we acknowledge and applaud the untiring work of the RSPCA. Remember it all started with a small coffee bean.

26th June

Breaking the Fast
> *"Go to a gossips' feast, and joy with me.*
> *After so long grief, such festivity."*
> > *(Comedy of Errors:* Act V: Scene 1.*)*

Tonight four friends will celebrate the birthday of someone very special to each of us, by preparing and eating a meal together. We will be observing the rules on social distancing, of course, but it will still be closer than we've been for three months. Zoom, Skype, WhatsApp, texts, social media, phone calls and even snail mail have all helped keep people in touch, and they've been a lifeline, but this moment of sharing food, drink and fellowship will be the real thing. The loyalty and laughter of friends: food for the soul.

27th June

A grim anniversary slipped under the radar last week:

World Refugee Day
A combination of war, violence and terror had already presented us with a global crisis. And then Covid-19 was added to the mix, compounding the problem. Everyone acknowledges there is an emergency. Getting consensus is trickier. Opinions are polarised. Many of us have entrenched views. In his poem 'Refugees', Brian Bilston examines the binary responses to this complex issue. He invites us to view

things from a different perspective, by reading the poem twice: first, conventionally from top to bottom; and then from the last line, working up to the beginning. The result is extraordinary and challenging. Look it up and give it a go.

28th June

"Let me not to the marriage of true minds admit impediments…"

I was a pageboy at my cousin Lillian's wedding. I think I must have been about five years old at the time. All that I can remember about the day is that we were driven to the church in a black Hackney cab; and that my fellow pageboy didn't share in my relish of the role, and grizzled all the way. By the time the group photo was snapped on the steps, I think his mood had affected mine. He manages a weak smile, while I look a little glum. A year or so later I'm captured by the camera again; this time presenting 'Aunty' Joyce with a lucky horseshoe at her marriage to 'Uncle' Peter, and look far more cheerful.

Fast-forward to the seventies and I graduate from bit-player to best man. John Wesker, the Rev Robert Williams and my brother Steve all asked me to play this vital role. I'm pleased to report I always produced the rings on cue, and that my speeches always spared the grooms' blushes. All three couples presented me with cufflinks as a token of thanks and a souvenir of the occasion.

Sometimes I've been asked to sing. For Veronica and Tony it

was 'How Great Thou Art'; for Cec and Bob, '*Bugeilio'r Gwenith Gwyn*'; while for John and Myfanwy there was only one choice, Joseph Parry's matchless love song, bearing that girl's name.

When Jen and Tim got married, five of us sang at the service in St Mary's Hanwell, and after a swift half-a-mile sprint, donned our aprons and served the wedding breakfast of our own home-made food in the Church Hall.

A wide range of contributions to nuptials, then. But since the Millennium there has been an unexpected twist: I've been invited to be the celebrant.

It first came about when Becky, the company stage manager on my solo show, *The Gospel According to John*, asked me to officiate at her marriage to Justin in Urquhart Castle on the shores of Loch Ness. Well, she knew I had a carrying voice from hearing my performances in vast cathedrals like Winchester and Wells; and that the costume I had worn would fit the bill perfectly. A Highland Wedding in the most romantic of settings, followed by a ceilidh in Drumnadrochit Village Hall. "Joyous!" Or as Simon Callow said in *Four Weddings and a Funeral*, "Brigadoon!"

Justin's mother Alison Skelton penned 'The Watergate of Castle Urquhart' for the occasion:

Now here's a song of high romance, this fortress
In a senseless place: Why build a castle down a hill?
Pitch camp where dragons play? Keep faith amidst
The faithless? Make this folly, marriage, still?

Who comes this way, the narrow way, comes by the
*   water gate:*

Past battlements of pride, of fear, past serpents of distrust,
Past whirlpools of deceit, past siren songs of lust,
We'll lash our wheel and hold our star: for love's the
      water gate.

For love! The old high splendid cause. Hold fast
The holy ship of fools! We nail our colours to the mast
Of sweet fidelity! High King of Heaven, bless the keep,
Bless the ship. Bless the dragons in their sleep.
Cast off, set course, make joyful way!
My soul and your soul are setting sail today.

The vows that followed were heartfelt, and a public declaration of the promises Becky and Justin had pledged at a private legal ceremony in Oxford Registry Office weeks before.

Years later, my delightful neighbours David and Kelly asked me to be a witness at their civil union in Ealing Town Hall. A great privilege. This was a very quiet affair, unlike the weekend-long celebration in the atmospheric ruins of Leiston Abbey in Suffolk months later. The robes had another airing. This couple's matrimonial promises were just as moving and spontaneous as those made in the Scottish rites years before. David and Kelly wrote their vows independent of each other, in separate rooms, without prior discussion. When they were recited they were uncannily similar in both tone and phraseology. Two became one.

I've made many friendships in my acting career. None firmer, fonder or more enduring than that with Gaynor and Nick Fraser. We all met on *Oliver!* in 1983. Those two fell in love and married. Over the years I've watched their three children grow up. Their eldest, Sophie, and her fiancé, Alisdair, asked me to do the honours at their nuptials a year ago today in Castelladral, near Barcelona. They are expecting a new arrival in the near future, with the promise of a christening sometime next year, once we have seen the back of Covid-19, hopefully.

Marriage is one of the greatest acts of faith there is; and now, more than ever. It has cheered me up no end that six friends of mine are planning to tie the knot next year and the year after. "God willing," as my mother always said; and now I add, "Corona permitting."

My services have been enlisted again.

My robes are not going to be mothballed just yet.

29th June

Short advice for a *long* marriage.
Al and Daz asked me to read a poem at their wedding.

"Make it a short one," they said.

Ogden Nash and I obliged. His poem is called 'A Word to Husbands'. It's very funny, and very brief. Just twenty-one words in total. Sadly, I can't quote it here for copyright reasons, but do have a gander. And a guffaw. Silence *is* golden.

30th June

Landmarks
I've been reading a psalm a day since lockdown started. Today I reach Psalm 100. It is upbeat in tone and short:

Psalm 100

A Psalm of Praise

Make a joyful noise unto the Lord, all ye lands.
Serve the Lord with gladness: come before his presence
with singing.
Know ye that the Lord, he is God:
It is he that hath made us,
And not we ourselves;
We are his people,
And the sheep of his pasture.
Enter into his gates with thanksgiving,
And into his courts with praise:
Be thankful unto him, and bless his name.
For the Lord is good, his mercy is everlasting;
And his truth endureth to all generations.

Today we've arrived at the end of another *lost* month. In my anthology, the poem for 30th June is by Alfred Lord Tennyson: 'Ulysses'. (I must say I prefer the Greek form of that name, 'Odysseus'.) But it's a stirring poem, and has resonances for us at this moment as we come to terms with the consequences of being confined to our own quarters. Odysseus, refusing to retire, believes:

How dull it is to pause, to make an end,
To rust unburnish'd, not to shine in use!

The poem runs to over seventy lines, so I won't reproduce it in full, just the concluding section, which reflects how we might feel as we creep out of our dark corners, world-wards, onwards and upwards, blinking into the light.

Old age hath yet his honour and his toil;
Death closes all: but something ere the end,
Some work of noble note, may yet be done,
Not unbecoming men that strove with Gods.
The lights begin to twinkle from the rocks:
The long day wanes: the slow moon climbs: the deep
Moans round with many voices, Come, my friends,
'Tis not too late to seek a newer world.
Push off, and sitting well in order smite
The sounding furrows; for my purpose holds
To sail beyond the sunset, and the baths
Of all the western stars, until I die.
Though much is taken, much abides; and though
We are not now that strength which in old days
Moved earth and heaven, that which we are, we are;
One equal temper of heroic hearts,
Made weak by time and fate, but strong in will
To strive, to seek, to find, and not to yield.

The Three Mousecateers v. Covid Cat

FIVE

JULY – THE CROWN OF THE YEAR

July has been called the *Crown* of the Year. *This* year the crown is tarnished.

1st July

Better Late than Never

My cousin Jill celebrated her eighty-second birthday yesterday. Born and bred in Swansea, Jill Francis left the 'Land of her Fathers' in the late 1950s to stay with cousins in Sault, Canada. While she was there she met a young American called Mick Hardley. They fell for each other and got hitched. In October this year they will have been married sixty-two years. During that time the family has increased greatly. At the latest count: *5* children; *14* grandchildren – though one lost in tragic circumstances and far too young, leaving *13*; and *10* great-grandchildren.

I have already extolled her virtues in the entry for 10th

May. On top of all her other qualities, Jill was blessed with stunning good looks. When she left these shores she also left behind a few broken hearts. In the six decades since then, her beautiful soul has won many admirers that side of the Atlantic. An export of which Wales can be proud.

2nd July

Roman Remains

Everything's a little behind at the moment. Today I get June's newsletter, a month late, about the progress of the Brentford Project. As I write we have only half a High Street. The south side has been flattened. Bank, post office, florist, baker, bike shop, nail bar, curry house: all gone. When the development is completed, there will be 800 new homes, 14,000 sq m. of commercial space, an extended Thames path; and lanes leading to the river will connect the town to the Thames once more. That link was lost due to choking industrialisation. The pace of the work has slackened during the pandemic, of course; but archaeologists have been on site, painstakingly revealing layers of Brentford past; and they have uncovered several Roman remains, including pieces of pottery and a well-preserved stone sarcophagus.

After reading this update, I walk to what is left of the High Street and take a picture of Brentford's monument: a granite pillar which commemorates, among other historical events, the battle Julius Caesar and his legions fought, and won, on this spot in 54 BC. He crossed the Thames here and gave it the name it has worn ever since. This reminds me of the poem the then poet laureate, Carol Ann Duffy, wrote on the occasion of our Queen's Diamond Jubilee. Old Father Thames hasn't had such a doughty champion since William Wordsworth composed his 'Ode on Westminster Bridge' in 1802. That poet laureate would be sad to know that the city's 'ships, towers, domes, theatres and temples' are all standing empty at this moment in our history, closed by Covid-19, but he would no doubt be cheered by the immutable presence of our river, the mighty Thames, the beating heart of London.

(Do take the time to read Carol Ann Duffy's homage to the river in her fine poem: 'The Thames'. I can guarantee you will not be disappointed.)

3rd July

"Tomorrow to fresh woods and pastures new..."

Yesterday a blow was redoubled. Having lost my agent two weeks ago, I receive an unwelcome email. The suspended tour of *The Mousetrap* will not be resuming. Not this year or next. What we'd all hoped would be merely postponement has turned out to be cancellation. This is so sad. It was a terrific production with a splendid cast. I feel very much for the younger members of the company with their careers before them: no prospect of immediate work, crippling student debt and little financial security. Let's hope there is some intervention soon to support the arts in general, and save our precious theatres in particular.

Although I've clocked up more than three score years and ten, I am as hungry as ever for work. The creative urge remains as strong as it was when I began this mad adventure in October 1977 at the Kenneth More Theatre, Ilford. So this morning I send off an email to an agency that has expressed an interest in representing me, and I will continue to explore new avenues of employment.

Today's readings offer encouragement.

From Psalm 103 there's a promise of a fresh start: "Thy youth is renewed like the eagle's."

While 'Solitude' by Ella Wheeler Wilcox recommends a positive approach:

Laugh, and the world laughs with you;
Weep, and you weep alone;
For the sad old earth must borrow its mirth,
But has trouble enough of its own.
Sing, and the hills will answer;
Sigh, it is lost on the air;
The echoes bound to a joyful sound,
But shrink from voicing care.

Rejoice, and men will seek you;
Grieve, and they turn and go;
They want full measure of all your pleasure,
But they do not need your woe.
Be glad, and your friends are many;
Be sad, and you lose them all, –
There are none to decline your nectared wine,
But alone you must drink life's gall.

Feast, and your halls are crowded;
Fast, and the world goes by.
Succeed and give, and it helps you live,
But no man can help you die.
There is room in the halls of pleasure
For a large and lordly train,
But one by one we must all file on
Through the narrow aisles of pain.

4th July

Independence Day

Today I send a love letter to all my family and friends on the other side of 'the Pond'. The prayer, 'God Bless America', is needed now more than ever. I add the inevitable postscript:

Stay well;

Keep safe.

5th, 6th and 7th July

Metro-Land

Yesterday was a sort of 'Independence Day' here at home, as a few of the lockdown restrictions have been relaxed. I take advantage and decide to spend the weekend with my friend Annie in *Metro-Land*. That was the name the poet John Betjeman gave that part of Bucks. He was a great railway enthusiast. I wonder what he would have made of HS2? Mixed feelings, I imagine. Certainly, he would have been impelled to write something on the subject.

On the Saturday morning, before breakfast, I pop into the garden, still in dressing gown and slippers, and pick a colanderful of plump, juicy raspberries. Fresh, with yoghurt and toasted oats, they make a healthy start to the day.

Later, I make my first attempt at making raspberry-ripple ice cream. The churn is put to chill in the freezer. I assemble the ingredients: condensed milk, eggs, vanilla pods, double cream and the starring berries. I google a few recipes and eventually decide to go solo and rely on instinct. What could possibly go wrong?

I take a leaf out of my mum's book – and Delia Smith's – and pray!

On Sunday, Annie and I go to Shardeloes, on the outskirts of Amersham, where suburbia meets the green belt. On the shores of Uncle John's lake, Evan and Min – Annie's son and daughter-in-law – are camping with their two boys, Rex, six, and Wilf, three. Two other families have joined them. They've paid no heed to the abruptly autumnal weather with its high winds and squally showers. The Turners and Hamilton-Pikes are made of stronger stuff. Tents are firmly pitched. Dogs are mock fighting. A tiny pug puppy, punching above its weight, is tormenting a playful, indulgent Springer Spaniel, three times its size. Eggs are frying over the fire. A young lad, all of seven, has a go on the slackline, showing fine circus skills and good balance. Wilf is driving his Dad's car: "Vroom, vroom! Vroom, vroom!"

We oldies turn down the offered wine and opt for a walk along the wooded shore to the boathouse, padlocked and razor-wired against thieves. Purple buddleia, a summer sister to the lilac of the spring, tempts the butterflies. We name the

Admirals Red and the Cabbage White, but there are showy Peacocks, too, and Painted Ladies, brazen and blousy on a Sunday afternoon. Dragonflies skim over the water and land at our feet, shining in the sudden sun. The brambles are thick with blossom and bowing with clusters of hard green berries, promising good pickings come September. Walking onto the pontoon, we gaze over the vast stretch of mirror-water, toward the island copse, a half-mile distant. Annie tells me of the losing battle the rainbow trout are waging against the water lice. Turning back, we spot a discarded beer can in the water, trapped among the reeds. We try to retrieve it with a fallen branch, but it sinks further beyond our reach.

Back around the campfire, we sit awhile, then, touching elbows and kissing air, make our goodbyes and take our leave. A chicken stuffed with haggis is calling; *and deep in the freezer, raspberry-ripple ice cream is waiting to be dressed with coulis and crowned with meringue.*

For me, having reached a certain age, home comforts have more appeal than the call of the wild. Meat and two veg on a plate, with gravy, a napkin and a knife and fork to hand, at a table indoors, win every time over a hot dog in a bun by a smoky fire on a blustery day. Time to put on my slippers. I have become thoroughly domesticated. Now I'm nesh! But I did enjoy my brush with nature; "Truly rural!" as my friend Frank from up Bude, used to say. And that wasn't easy, as he had a weak 'R'!

Waking on Monday morning I close my eyes again and retrace yesterday's restorative walk, picturing again the beeches, oaks, horse chestnuts and willows that fringe the lake at Shardeloes.

A Haiku insinuates itself into my musings:

I Talk to the Trees

> *We talk of the trees*
> *as the lungs of our planet.*
> *"Please breathe for us now."*

8th July

"For this relief, much thanks."
News of the Government's £1.57 billion boost to the arts is most welcome. It follows concerted and unprecedented lobbying of ministers and MPs. The pressure has paid off. Sadly, it has come too late to save theatres like Southampton's Nuffield and Leicester's Haymarket. Our tour of *The Mousetrap* was one of the latest casualties, putting twenty of us out of work.

Let's hope this state funding will reach all regions, and the benefits will be felt as far away as Truro, Inverness, Coleraine and Milford Haven; and that it will filter down from the elite institutions at the top to the grassroots.

On a personal level I have been touched by the expressions of goodwill I have received on the loss of my livelihood and the retirement of my agent, the lovely Lisa. I'm glad to say I have found a new agent, or rather he found me. That was good for self-esteem. I feel a corner has been turned.

10th July

"I must go down to the sea again…"

The question is, "When?"

This week 'The Good Ship Mousetrap' should have docked in Swansea. Naturally, I am disappointed not to see friends and family at the Grand Theatre. Many of them had booked their tickets months ago. I was looking forward to: staying with my brother, sister-in-law and the two dogs; eating a salty-sweet, peppery treat – Penclawdd cockles – from a bag, while mooching around Swansea Market; taking an hour-long walk from Town to Mumbles along the Prom; calling on chums in Chapel Street; perhaps a portion of chips from Johnny's; and finishing in Joe's art deco ice-cream parlour for the second indulgence of the day – a 'North Pole', topped with chocolate vermicelli *and* nibbles of mixed nuts. For the moment, paradise must be postponed.

While these thoughts of Swansea preoccupy me, I think of a favourite song from Cadle schooldays:

'Farewell to you my Nancy'. Verse three sums up the current situation perfectly:

For now the storm is rising, I see it coming on;
The night is dark as anything, we cannot see the moon.
Our good old ship, she is tossed aft, our rigging is all tore.
But still I live in hope to see old Swansea Town once more.
Old Swansea Town once more, fine girl, you're the girl
that I adore.
But still I live in hope to see Old Swansea Town once
more.

12th July

The Show Must Go On

A rare night of rain in the summer of 1976. The Questors had brought its production of Anouilh's *The Lark* from Ealing to The Minack on the Cornish coast. The threatening storm broke halfway through the first performance. This was such bad timing. The days leading up to the opening had been unbelievably hot, with hours of sunshine and cloudless skies. But not that July evening. Distant thunder was soon followed by relentless rain. And we had barely started. Ten minutes into the downpour and the electrics failed. We couldn't see each other on stage. And the audience were in the dark too. But not for long. Having donned waterproof protection, the seasoned playgoers turned on their torches and shone them directly at us. One problem solved by resourcefulness. But there was another and more pressing one. There was no sound system. And the coronation of the Dauphin was fast approaching, with the recessional underscored with music by Poulenc. What to do? Then, Alison Pollard, playing Joan of Arc, had the presence of mind to break the growing pause after the crowning by proclaiming, "God save the King! God save the King!" Relieved, the rest of the cast took up the cry, saving the day. The director was so impressed, he decided to keep it in for the subsequent performances.

By the time the matinee started next day, normal service was restored. The sun was blazing again. When we reached the trial scene, we interrogators were facing not only Joan but also the blinding glare of the sun, and the equally strong reflection of the rays off the granite stage and cliffs. It was impossible to keep both eyes open. There was nothing for it: the inquisitors winked at the accused, inappropriately.

Why am I sharing this anecdote? Well, it was stirred by the news that this magical amphitheatre last night welcomed back its audience for the first time this year. Rowena Cade, who eighty years ago carved this arena out of the granite cliffs with her own hands, would have been proud. I have an enduring memory of her in a frayed sloppy Joe and gumboots, sitting on an upturned wheelbarrow, surveying the action from her clifftop perch.

A woman of vision, grit and determination. And what a memorial she has left behind.

Where The Minack has led, may other venues follow. And soon.

The show *will* and *must* go on.

14th July

The times they are a-changin…
I see a man walking his dog in the park:
not unusual.
There is a family resemblance:
that's normal, surely?
They both have grey hair,
and share an air
of cool detachment.
But here's a funny thing:
the master is muzzled;
the mutt is not.

As we cross paths,
do I catch
a canine grin?

15th July

Safety in Numbers
The starlings are back.
Not for the cherries now.
Numbering a dozen
they bully a blackbird
looking for early worms
after dawn rain.
The circle tightens
Until,
Outnumbered,
The darker stranger
Concedes,
gives ground,
flies home.
The pack pecks on
Until,
Sensing menace,
Unseen yet real,
Instant sanctuary
is sought
and found
in the familiar Cherry tree.

16th July

"Is there a Pasteur in the House?"

Today marks the anniversary of Pasteur's successful development of a vaccine against rabies. Just one of his many achievements. I picked up my pinta to pour on my cereal this morning and thought of the great scientist. As I held the carton that bears the name for the overfamiliar, taken-for-granted process that makes the milk safe to drink, I gave thanks. Feeling bold, I eschewed my usual green-top – semi-skimmed – and opted for the blue – whole, full-fat and *pasteurised*. Don't talk to me, by the way, of the abomination that is topped with red: skimmed. "See-through", I call it. Unspeakable.

How we need a Pasteur at the moment to come up with a vaccine or a cure for Covid-19. When it comes, let's hope the knowledge will be shared universally, and the treatment will be free for all.

17th July

Raising a Glass

Last night I had my first dinner guests since rules were relaxed. My friends Beryl and Anthony were welcomed into my bubble. I was determined to make it a special occasion. The best cloth and napkins: laundered, starched and ironed; the canteen raided for the posh, polished cutlery; the finest cut-glass goblets and tumblers glistened at each place. They're very special as they're Waterford Crystal, which is no longer made. My Irish great-grandparents came from that part of the world. As I lay the table, I think of my dad's mother, Grandma Francis (nee Walsh), my Irish forebears, and also my friends James and Meic who gave me these beautiful glasses.

A gift that certainly keeps on giving.

When we sit to eat, a heartfelt grace is given: for food, for friends and the restoration of fellowship.

"*After so long fast, such festivity.*"

18th July

Poetry is Power

Today would have been Nelson Mandela's 102nd birthday. The freedom-fighter spent twenty-seven years in prison, many in solitary confinement. Apparently his warder welcomed him to his cell with the words:

"This is Robben Island. This is where you will die."

Like Churchill before him, and Obama after, Mandela quoted from 'Invictus' following his election as the first president of a free South Africa. The poem had given him solace and strength during his long walk to freedom.

Invictus
by W.E. Henley

> *Out of the night that covers me*
> *Black as the pit from pole to pole,*
> *I thank whatever gods may be*
> *For my unconquerable soul.*

In the fell clutch of circumstance
I have not winced nor cried aloud.
Under the bludgeonings of chance
My head is bloody but unbowed.

Beyond this place of wrath and tears
Looms but the Horror of the shade,
And yet the menace of the years
Finds and shall find me unafraid.

It matters not how strait the gate,
How charged with punishments the scroll,
I am the master of my fate,
I am the captain of my soul.

At his trial Mandela had spoken eloquently about the struggle against the evil of Apartheid. He and his cohorts were prepared to pay the ultimate sacrifice for their cause. His stance was reminiscent of Edith Cavell when she said before her execution: "I have seen death so often that it is not strange or fearful to me."

During his incarceration Nelson found the works of Shakespeare a comfort. The following lines from *Julius Caesar* hit home:

Cowards die many times before their deaths;
The valiant never taste of death but once.
Of all the wonders that I yet have heard,
It seems to me most strange that men should fear,
Seeing that death, a necessary end,
Will come when it will come.

Poetry will never lose its power to console, to challenge and to inspire. We would be lost without it and much the poorer.

19th July

Keeping Pace

This morning I ran a marathon. I knew it had been coming for a while so I was in prime condition. I'd been in training for a hundred and eighteen days. Today I reach Psalm 119. It has 176 verses in all. Almost a quarter of an hour's reading. The previous two days weren't ideal preparation: Psalm 117 is a sprint, comprising two short verses; 118, with twenty-nine, is more of a middle-distance race.

The psalms, of course, are meant to be sung. If 117 could be called a short hymn and 118 a lengthy anthem, then 119 must qualify as an oratorio. Three of the greatest examples of this genre, Haydn's *Creation*, Mendelssohn's *Elijah* and Handel's *Messiah* all draw heavily on the Book of Psalms. Brahms, too, found rich pickings for his *German Requiem*; and Bernstein set several of them, using the original Hebrew texts, in his *Chichester Psalms*. Hubert Parry's thunderous anthem, 'I Was Glad' has been sung at every coronation since Edward VII's in 1902. That is a setting of the first six verses of Psalm 122, which will be along in three days' time. Before then I will have to face 'the sharp arrows of the mighty' (Psalm 120) and 'lift up mine eyes unto the hills' (Psalm 121).

In fact, it's well worth quoting more of the uplifting lines from that psalm:

He will not suffer thy foot to be moved:
He that keepeth thee will not slumber.
The sun shall not strike thee by day,
Nor the moon by night.

I have found the psalms have proved to be a good workout for the mind, soul and spirit.

20th July

Do we expect too much of our leaders? If past 'heroes' were subjected to forensic, posthumous examination, would they too be found wanting? Churchill famously remarked: "History will be kind to me, for I intend to write it."

My poem explores this theme.

Fallen Icon

They got it wrong,
The Ancients,
when blinded by wonder
and reflected light,
they thought the rays
around the Sun-god's head
were made of gold.
His legs were trunks of iron
brazen-clad.
A heart of stone.

Below ground
faults, rocks and plates
Collide.
Colossus collapses,
brought down to earth
and piecemeal
scattered
into the Aegean.
Examining the remains
the scholars of Rhodes
on second sight
conclude:
"His feet weren't
bronze at all,
but made of clay."

21st July

Bish! Bash! Bosh!

Ben Stokes has done it again: turned a Test Match on its head, and set up an unlikely England win in Old Trafford. Pure *Boys' Own*. What a contrast with two years ago when he was involved in a brawl outside a bar in Bristol. He has certainly come of age since that brush with the law. His rehabilitation is complete. An all-round cricketing hero. Good news on the sporting field is just the tonic we need at the moment. A welcome distraction. More of the same, please, Ben.

Well done, that man.

22nd July

All the King's – and Queen's – Men

A few months after London emerged from plague in 1602, the first Elizabethan age ended and the Jacobean began with the accession of James I. One of his first acts, even before he was crowned, was to give royal patronage to The Chamberlain's Men, a company headed by Burbage and Shakespeare. From that time forward they were to be known as The King's Men. The Royal Warrant recognised the huge store set by live performance.

"Theatre was," said the King, "all for our solace and pleasure."

This funding meant the company could perform all year round: the summer, outdoors in The Globe: the winter, indoors at the Blackfriars Playhouse.

The Red Bull in Clerkenwell, a converted inn-yard, also found favour at court. The Queen gave it her backing. This was an acknowledgement of the power of comedy to lift the spirits and bring much-needed joy in those days when death was never far away. In fact, in the first ten years of James' reign, the theatres were closed for a total of seventy-eight months, because of further outbreaks of plague.

When I was a primary school teacher in the seventies, history was one of the most popular subjects I taught. And the favourite period was the Tudors and Stuarts. I can still remember two hilarious howlers from my pupils' writings:

On the pestilence:

"Many people left London, hopping not to catch the plague."

On the first Stuart monarch:

"James I had protruding eyes, which ran in the family."

It was said of that king that he was "the wisest fool in Christendom". Posterity can certainly applaud him for his support of theatre, and for instigating a new translation of the scriptures: the *Authorised Version*, which is still affectionately referred to as the *King James Bible*. There is a theory that Shakespeare was responsible for the psalms. I like to think that is the case.

True or not, the English language certainly flourished in the Jacobean age.

23rd July

Red Kop v. Red Top
After thirty years of heartache, Liverpool A.F.C. are worthy champions of the League once more. And what a way to celebrate with a carnival of a match against Chelsea. A 5–3 thriller. A grand finale to a bizarre season, and a great advert for the beautiful game. Sadly, the Kop and the rest of the stadium was empty.

This success was hard won and was all the sweeter because of the Covid hiatus. Liverpool came close to gaining the top spot last season so this achievement is testimony to their consistency. They deserved this.

Last night was a far cry from the tragic events of 15th April 1989, and the years of struggle since the Hillsborough

Disaster. The survivors and relatives of the victims have fought long and hard for truth, justice and closure.

The bald facts:
96 fatalities
766 injuries

A litany of failures by the police, the press and politicians. Within hours of the abandonment of the match, the police fed the press false stories claiming that hooliganism and drunkenness by Liverpool fans was the cause. Bernard Ingham, Mrs Thatcher's doctor of spin, helped spread the misinformation, branding the supporters "tanked-up yobs". Years later when the inquest jury exonerated them from all blame, Sir Bernard, as he was then, refused to change his opinion, let alone apologise.

At least Kelvin MacKenzie, the editor of the *Sun* at the time, apologised for his newspaper's reprehensible coverage of the tragedy. The morning after the disaster it ran the headline: 'THE TRUTH', having toyed with the idea of going with: 'YOU SCUM!'

In a way what they opted for was more subversive and inflammatory than the first idea. The article which followed the headline bore no resemblance to the truth.

According to the 'Red Top', the fans:

- picked the pockets of victims;
- urinated on 'our brave cops';
- and, beat up a constable while he was giving the kiss of life to an injured man.

All lies.

After the inevitable backlash from thousands of Liverpudlians, the then editor of the *Sun* approached Kenny Dalglish, Liverpool's manager, to ask how he could repair the damage his tabloid had done.

"How's about 'WE LIED!' as your front-page headline, tomorrow," was the suggestion that came back. Of course that didn't happen. It took another twenty-three years before they apologised unreservedly. By then it was too little, too late. There are thousands of Scousers who still boycott the *Sun*.

Not only do Liverpool play some of the best football, but they have the finest anthem as well: 'You'll Never Walk Alone'. And when they sing it they mean every word. They have braved 'the wind and the rain'; and now, at last, can bask under that longed-for 'golden sky'.

Well done, lads. You have made not just your great city proud, but the whole country as well.

And to the *Sun*, fans of the Reds could be forgiven for saying, in the word of another of its notorious headlines:

GOTCHA!

24th July

Red for Ruth Day

A poignant moment at Old Trafford this morning: Sir Andrew Strauss and his two sons rang the five-minute bell to summon England and West Indies onto the field of play for the first day of the final Test. The ex-England opener, former captain and director of cricket was dressed in a red suit with matching tie; his two boys in red baseball caps and T-shirts. When the players emerged from the pavilion, both sides were wearing red caps on their heads and numbers on their backs. This was a mark of respect for Ruth Strauss, Andrew's late wife and mother to Samuel and Luca, who died from a rare form of lung cancer two years ago at the age of forty-six. She had never smoked.

'Red for Ruth Day' was inaugurated last year during the Lords' Test against Australia and raised over half a million pounds. That occasion was attended by a full house of over 28,000: yesterday the stands, of course, were empty.

Research into deaths from lung cancer unrelated to smoking continues. The cause hasn't gone away just because of the Coronavirus pandemic.

The hunt to find a cure for all forms of cancer continues.

July 25th and 26th July

When Neighbours Become Good Friends
My new neighbours, Yvonne and Joseph, got married today. Although I've only known them for six weeks, we are on Christian-name terms already. But I was surprised when they invited me to the wedding reception in their back garden. A pleasant and kind gesture. The weather was far from kind, however. It stair-rodded most of the afternoon. Fortunately, they were well prepared for the vagaries of high summer weather in the UK. They have lived here long enough to know

how unreliable our climate is. Joseph was born in Ghana but came here in his teens. Yvonne's family come from Sierra Leone, but she was born in Blighty. Joseph, with the help of his two brothers, had spent the best part of the last week erecting four gazebos in the garden, so quite a large area was under cover. Just as well, as the rain was relentless. Joseph looked very dapper in a blue three-piece suit while Yvonne was stunning in a cream lace bridal gown. She did her best to keep the full skirt out of the mud, but eventually gave in and changed into a bronze number which was less likely to show the brown slurry stains. Seeing some of the traditional West African costumes worn by the guests and tasting the delicious regional cuisine on offer reminded me of the very happy times I spent in Sierra Leone and Ghana between 1977 and 1982 for the British Council. (My friend Eleanor and I made three tours there performing two-hander versions of Shakespeare's plays round schools, universities and colleges. There are enough tales of our adventures to fill another book, but that's one that Eleanor should write as she sensibly kept a detailed diary.)

Back to the wedding celebration. After being cooped up for months, everyone was determined to have a good time. We ate. We drank. We chatted, sang and danced. There were speeches. And lots of laughter. The rain did not dampen our spirits. WAWA... West Africa Wins Again!

This is turning out to be quite a neighbourly weekend. After Saturday's nuptials, Sunday brings a belated birthday celebration. David, who lives with his wife Mary on the other side of the street, had a significant birthday in April. That was at the height of the pandemic, and there hasn't been much of a chance to mark the event until now. Together with Peter from number 26 we all walk in the Sunday sun to The Express Tavern a mile away, near Kew Bridge. David has booked a table for four in the newly constructed conservatory, ultra-modern and very impressive. It's more of a glass box really, and with its sliding doors and retractable roof is ready for all weathers. Today we're fortunate as the roof and walls are open as far as they can go. David announces before we look at the menu, or order our first round of drinks, that he is picking up the tab for everything. We protest that we should all be treating him, but he insists that he's 'in the chair'. There is the usual range of roasts on offer but we all plump for the beef. We are not disappointed. Each plate has a generous helping of tender sirloin, a variety of seasonal vegetables and is topped with a Yorkshire pud as big as an Ascot hat. And lots of RBG… rich, brown gravy. Delicious. We even find room for dessert. The greedier opt for sticky toffee pudding and custard, the more abstemious can only manage a sorbet. The walk home is much slower as we are all carrying extra weight! When we turn into Mafeking Avenue, Mary presses us to liqueurs and we don't need any arm-twisting. An end to a perfect day spent in good company.

29th July

Kew

This is the third visit since Kew reopened its gates. Jane and I meet at 9.45am under threatening skies. Masked and socially distanced, we chat in the queue, waiting for the 10.00am opening. After flashing e-tickets and membership cards, we gel our hands and make our way to one of our favourite haunts, under a huge copper beech tree, near the humming Hive, a stunning installation triggered by the local bees. We sit, share our news of the past week, eat our breakfast picnic, drink our coffee from our thermos flasks and have a go at Monday's *Guardian* crossword. Just before we leave, Jane takes me on a short detour. She insists there's something I "must see!" – Simon Gudgeon's extraordinary sculpture, 'Leaf Spirit', made in bronze from the imprints of leaves. A mask we can all enjoy. Its beauty is breathtaking. I make a silent vow: I will return to view it again and again. For the moment I take its picture like a snap-happy tourist.

30th July

Eye Test

It seems to me that once you hit the age of seventy you start to lose all sense of time. I get a reminder from the opticians that my eye test is due. I cannot believe it. I'm sure I got new specs, at enormous expense, a few short months ago. But you can't argue with Boots. They know best. And they want my money. To be fair it doesn't pay to take any risks with the precious gift of sight, so I book an appointment, but decide I won't be tempted to spend too much this time. After the optometrist conducts a thorough examination the optician does the hard sell to flog me varifocals. I argue that I tried a pair years ago and couldn't get on with them. She presses on, insisting that the technology has improved. I blanch when she mentions the price. *How much?*

The technical advances are surely not worth that price tag.

I'm a pensioner with no other source of income and cannot justify that sort of expenditure. We reach a compromise in the end. As I have astigmatism and the start of cataracts, the optometrist convinces me that I need distance glasses as well as my usual readers. I resist at first arguing that I don't drive, rarely go to the cinema – that's not going to happen anytime soon is it? – and don't watch that much TV. A fortnight later when I receive my new specs I have to agree that the picture on my telly is much clearer with distance glasses, and that they were necessary after all, in spite of my misgivings.

£250 well spent.

31st July

Happy Hour at Holly's
The month is rounded off by a visit to Mortlake and happy hour in Holly's garden, at the stipulated distance of two metres. Getting there is as enjoyable as the get-together itself. A ten-minute journey on a spacious, almost empty train from Brentford to Barnes Bridge, followed by one of my favourite walks, on the river bank. Walking westward towards the sun setting in the Thames behind the old brewery – trust me, it's more picturesque than it sounds – I can understand why Turner painted this view of the river.

As July closes I hope we may all be able to socialise more as we move from late summer into autumn and beyond.

July, the 'crown of the year', is slightly tarnished this time round.

Perhaps next year its lustre will be restored?

SIX

AUGUST – THE ENGLISH WINTER, ENDING IN JULY, TO RECOMMENCE IN AUGUST

The first of the month finds me looking in my diary, checking for upcoming engagements in my Filofax (yes, I still have one!) and it's encouraging to see there are a few social events pencilled in. Let's pray they'll be inked in shortly and not rubbed out. As I'm leafing through, out falls a shiny black cardboard pouch, bearing the motto:

THERE'S A LITTLE THEATRE IN US ALL.

Inside, there's a theatre voucher for £20, and another message:

YOU'VE BEEN GIVEN THE MAGICAL GIFT OF THEATRE. ENJOY THE SHOW!

I feel a lump rising in my throat, but I know I'm not alone; millions are missing live performance, and longing for it to return. And when it does we can put on our glad rags, and mark the occasion in style.

Three Bling Mice

Reality check.

The most exciting moment today is feeding the tomatoes with a solution of liquid seaweed. I really must get out more.

Before the day closes, I make a resolution. It's not January, of course, but this is not a conventional year. The resolution is: I will ration my Facebook posts from now on, as I'm going to edit them and put them into a book. I hold several friends responsible for nagging me into doing this. What have they started?

3rd August

It's a Girl!

My friends Sophie and Alisdair are parents for the first time; and it's a girl, weighing in at 7lb 1oz. It was a tricky labour and there are further complications. The baby is in isolation in the neonatal unit, and is being treated with antibiotics. All this before she has a name, or can be held in her parents' arms. There is a worrisome night for all the family, but better news in the morning. She is responding well, but her infection stats are still high, so she will remain on the maternity ward with Sophie until the week's course of medication is finished and she is infection-free.

And now she has a name: *Margot Rose.*

May she blossom and grow. She certainly belongs to a loving, caring family who will nurture her in the years ahead. Wasn't it just yesterday when her own mother was a week-old infant herself? How can this have happened so quickly? But then, "You're old, Father William!"

5th August

A Gem of a Friend

Isn't it grand when friends who haven't seen each other for

years are unexpectedly reunited? This happened to me last year when our tour of *The Mousetrap* played Malvern. After the Wednesday matinee a call came over the tannoy:

"Visitor at Stage Door for John Griffiths."

On such occasions you never know who or what is waiting. All you hope is that it's not going to interfere with the precious break before the evening show and that you will recognise, and *like*, the unexpected caller. When I get to the vestibule both those boxes are ticked: it's *Christine Wall* and I am very pleased to see her. She immediately reassures me that she won't keep me long as *I'm old and need to rest* – my words, not hers, but that's the subtext; and I'm thankful for her thoughtfulness. Not surprising really as she's a woman of the theatre herself and has a big heart. We first met when we were both working for Stewart Trotter on *Bless the Bride* at the Northcott, Exeter, in 1984. Twelve months later we were working together again in the opening rep season at the newly refurbished Everyman, Cheltenham, for John Doyle. Christine was Head of Wardrobe, and I've never met a better one. No surprise when after Cheltenham days she went to work for Alan Ayckbourn at the Stephen Joseph, Scarborough. Quite a CV. Premier League.

Back to that Wednesday last summer. Christine and I chat briefly. She tells me that she lives quite near in a country cottage with her husband, Mick, and that her surname is now Gemson. There will be more time to catch up and reminisce later in the week, for she invites me to lunch. I accept readily. Among her many other accomplishments, she's a brilliant cook, and a lapsed vegetarian she tells me, so that's even better.

Since that July reunion we have picked up the friendship with renewed vigour, only regretting that we lost touch for so many years. To compensate, Christine comes to stay for a few days to celebrate a 'round-figure' birthday in November 2019. She arrives bearing home-made treats. What my friend Liz calls 'latch-lifters'! I love that expression. Cornish, I think.

One of the tasks I found most onerous and stressful on the 2019 tour of *The Mousetrap* was booking my own accommodation each week. There were forty dates, so it took a lot of organising. On the 2020 tour, Christine did all the booking for me, for a small consideration. I felt a huge load had fallen off my back. All I had to do was sort out travel arrangements, and do eight shows a week. Quite enough for an old 'turn'. In the end, of course, I didn't need somewhere to stay after 16th March when the Corona curtain came down. During lockdown, Christine has been kept extremely busy around the charming cottage and in their productive garden. Lots of the fruit and veg are turned into delicious jams, jellies and chutneys; these are shared with neighbours and friends. She has also found time to make up scrubs for hard-pressed doctors and nurses. A few weeks ago she sent me a small stained-glass mobile in the NHS colours to hang in my window. The rainbow-ring refracts the sunlight and casts its cheerful, multicoloured beams on my wooden floor

When Christine arrives for lunch today, she doesn't come empty-handed. There is a jar of her own crab-apple jelly and another of plum jam, made only yesterday from actress Susie Blake's fruit. (Clang!)

There's also a mask in silk, patterned with foxes, that she's made for me. It's cooler and more comfy than the cotton variety. And chic.

Christine is a charming guest. We linger over lunch for three hours; and when it's time for her to leave so she can drive while it's still light and beat the worst of the traffic, it seems as if only ten minutes have passed. Making our goodbyes, we promise to keep in touch. *And this time I know we will.*

After clearing up and having a short siesta, I turn my thoughts to this evening's engagement. I've been invited to happy hour by my *Mousetrap* mucker, Susie Penhaligon. (Clang!) (That's two today. And both Susies. Stop it.) It's turned out nice again. I walk along the river path from Mafeking Avenue to The Admiral Tromp (that's with an 'o' not a 'u') – a Dutch barge next to Kew Bridge, which Susie, proud of her roots, always reminds me is made of Cornish granite. The bridge, not the boat, of course.

On an evening like this there's no better place to be than on Susie's deck, watching the sun go down with a sundowner. The end to a perfect day. But Susie and I would still prefer to have been in the theatre tonight telling stories to our supporters sitting in the dark. We're missing the magic of live theatre... and the money.

6th August

Hampstead for Lunch
I seem to be living entirely for pleasure at the moment. Perhaps I'm cramming in lots of engagements because of

the months of isolation, and also because there's the nagging thought that our new-found freedoms might be snatched away if the threatened *second spike* occurs. Perhaps, not wishing to be pessimistic, that should be *when,* not *if.* It's an easy journey to my friends Terry and Shirley King on Parliament Hill, a hundred yards from Hampstead Heath. A short bus ride to Gunnersbury Station is followed by a brief train trip to the bottom of their road. On the way up the steep hill to their door, I pass the Magdala Pub, boarded up and bleak. It was the scene of the tragic events of Easter Sunday, 10th April 1955, when Ruth Ellis, the last woman to be hanged in the UK, shot her lover, David Blakely, on the pavement outside. The wall still bears the bullet mark.

Great to see my Hampstead chums again. We met in the sixties at Swansea Little Theatre in Evelyn Burman-Jones' production of *Much Ado About Nothing.* In those days they were both teachers and I was training to be one. Shirley made a career change in the seventies, and after doing a one-year post-grad course at the Welsh College of Speech and Drama, joined the acting profession. I was inspired by this, and when the chance came for me to turn pro in 1977, I followed her example, if not strictly in her footsteps. I was offered a Provisional Equity card in rep, and learned on the job. Fortunately, there was a lot of work about then, though acting has always remained a precarious occupation; and more so now than ever. Shirley and I have worked together just the twice, and on each occasion it was in productions of *Under Milk Wood*: the first for BBC Radio 4 to mark the twenty-fifth anniversary of the first broadcast of this Play for Voices; and the second (*Clang* alert. Skip the next bit if I've given you tinnitus already) directed by Roger Michell for the National Theatre, with Ruth Jones and Rhys Ifans *before* they were famous in film and on TV. (*Clang! Clang! Clang!*)

As today is sunny we eat in the garden room. It's a case of 'Major Metcalf in the Conservatory with the Ham and Mustard'. We finish lunch with a rich Columbian coffee. That would, of course, be too wet on its own, so it comes with a slice of daughter Jessica's moist Lemon Drizzle. Knockout.

Homewards I go, happy and replete.

8th August

The Harveys in Hanwell

A garden party in the grounds of St Mellitus Church to celebrate the Golden Wedding Anniversary of Jane and Roy. A fitting setting as they are both committed and practical members of this church in the heart of Hanwell.

Jane and Roy were the first friends I made when I moved to Ealing to take up my teaching post in Stanhope Junior School, Greenford in September 1970. At that time they had only been married a matter of weeks. They lived in a delightful terraced house that backed onto the River Brent, in a leafy part of Hanwell. This is a very green area: Connolly Dell, Churchfields, and Brent Valley Golf Course are all nearby, as is the Wharncliffe Viaduct, one of Brunel's finest bridges on his Great Western Railway. I met the newly-weds, both teachers, through Rev Fred Secombe whom I'd known in Swansea when he'd had a parish there. He was now Rector of St Mary's Church and had already set up a Gilbert and Sullivan Society. After the weekly rehearsal Jane would often invite us back to the marital home in Half-Acre Road for coffee. And that's all it was in those days. A cup of instant: Nescafe or Maxwell House. Though some weeks we would adjourn following a thirsty, note-bashing, harmony-learning practice to the Park Hotel, gasping for a pint.

The next few years are full of music-making, and not just G & S, but at church services, the weddings of friends, Old Time Music Hall and carolling for charity each Christmas. Under the direction of our maestro, Meic, a musical martinet, we form the Anona Creedy Ensemble, which guarantees we have a very busy calendar and an active social life. Jane is the gel of the alto section. Roy doesn't sing, but is a great organiser of our events, making lists, shaking the collection boxes and totting up the totals we raise. And he is always generous with hospitality and giving lifts. He loves driving. All skills he learned in his previous career as a police officer with the Met, I suppose. Becoming disillusioned with their methods he changed direction and met Jane when they were both at teachers' training college. Romance, marriage and their son Rhodri all came later.

At today's celebration, marking the exact date of the nuptials fifty years ago, Rhodri and his wife Sheila are much in evidence. They are the driving force behind the party and have spent weeks planning it. They encouraged everyone to RSVP to the emailed invites in plenty of time, to help with the catering. And numbers have had to be restricted to thirty because of the pandemic. There are four gazebos in the spacious vicarage garden in case the weather takes a nasty turn. But the elements behave; the sun has got his hat on.

Hip,hip, hip, hooray! Son and daughter-in-law don't let up today either and make sure that everyone is looked after, fed and watered (and wined!). Charming hosts. And the three grandchildren, Luca, Mia and Kaya, are a delight. Rhodri proposes the toast to his parents and we guests oblige with: "Jane and Roy!" Much clapping, cheering and quaffing.

Jane responds on behalf of them both, "My husband and I..." Her speech is short, to the point and sincere. We all love it and re-echo our toast to the couple. Roy smiles contentedly. The smile of a man who knows he made a sound choice over half a century ago. I wonder if he's read 'A Word to Husbands' by Ogden Nash? I don't ask. Today of all days, 'silence is golden'. And the sun and the flowers agree.

12th August

Thoroughly Spoiled

Today is what I call Foot-and-Mouth Day: chiropody with Louisa across the road in Number 18. There are four patients in this morning's surgery: our hosts, Mary and David, Irene from number 22, and me. We are rewarded with tea and Tunnock biscuits once we've been under the knife, file and buffer. Louisa is very thorough and each individual treatment lasts an hour. You feel at the finish as if you have a new pair of feet. We all agree it's like walking on air.

Mary has another treat in store: lunch. One of her specialities is on today's menu. It's a pasta bake with meat sauce, topped with a light béchamel, enriched with beaten egg and dusted with grated cheese; served with refreshing

Greek salad *and* spicy potato wedges on the side. No one leaves the Carters' table feeling faint for lack of food.

'Foot-and-Mouth' comes around every six weeks. That's probably just as well: more frequent, and the waistline might disappear altogether.

13th August

Today was a day of two agents.

Just before 10.00am my ex-agent, Lisa Hull, calls for a chat. She tells me about the glorious holiday she and the family recently spent in Cornwall, the most relaxing she has spent in years, free as she is now of the worries of running her own business and the demands of her clients. Let's face it, actors are very demanding.

Then, just after 11.00am, I set off to meet my new agent, Simon Mayhew, at a Soho café where he is seeing clients and hopeful applicants all day. Each one allotted an hour. Except for yours truly, that is. Hungry for work – and food – I have opted for the lunchtime slot which "Simon says" will last two hours. I feel special. Although it is eleven years since we worked together on the tour of *Chitty*, we chat away as if the gap has been much shorter. It's a positive meeting: ideas, plans and ambitions are aired. But the Covid cloud is not far away.

'If' is suddenly a very big word indeed.

All we can do is wait and hope for the best. And eat.

13th & 14th August

Seeing More Clearly

Friday 13th proves to be lucky. Encouraged by my new agent, I have decided to try for more voice work. This seems a good time as we don't know when live theatre will return. My agent puts me in touch with a Voice agency called Crying Out Loud and I book a slot with them. In the first instance I have a very interesting conversation with Marina Calderone who is going to guide me through the process. Today the pieces she has selected for my voice reel arrive. Exciting.

On Saturday I pick up my new glasses from Boots, so there's no excuse now not to sit down and start studying these excerpts for my seminar with Marina in a fortnight's time. Then the shortlist will be whittled down to ten, ready for the recording in a Kennington studio in the middle of September

Reasons to be cheerful. As Dick Jones used to say: "Better to be optimistic than have a misty optic!"

17th August

Today sees me in a more serious vein. I go back to my new solicitor in Barnes to redraft my will and look into setting up Lasting Powers of Attorney, or 'eternity', as my mother insisted on saying. I have no wish to be maudlin, but as I live alone and have neither partner nor offspring, I think this is a wise move. My friends Kelly and David, who used to live next door, have agreed that I can lodge these powers with them. We have become like family. I'm lucky to have them in my life.

19th August

A Lockdown Landmark

Today I reach and read Psalm 150. The last one.

That equates to one hundred double-columned pages of small print in my large King James bible. Five months of reading and reflection.

The book starts with a psalm of calm meditation and beautiful imagery...

He shall be like a tree planted by the rivers of water,
that bringeth forth his fruit in his season;
his leaf also shall not wither;
and whatsoever he doeth shall prosper...

and ends on a high note, with music and dance. A mood of celebration:

Praise him with the sound of the trumpet... the psaltery
and harp... the timbrel and dance... stringed instruments
and organs... and loud cymbals.

If one verse encapsulates the whole experience for me it must be the pearl I found in verse 105 of the longest chapter, Psalm 119:

Thy word is a lamp unto my feet, and a light unto my path.

Much needed and appreciated in these days of darkness.

20th August

Out of the woodwork came a bookworm

The thing is, once you start posting on Facebook, you never know who is going to ♥, *Like* or *Comment*. I have acquired lots more friends through my daily jottings, and have heard from people I haven't seen in years. One of these is an ex-pupil whom I taught in Stanhope Junior School in the seventies, Leigh Fry. He's been enjoying my musings, and when I post that I'm thinking of publishing them in a book, he offers to help as that is his area of expertise. We have an hour-long chat which is full of sound advice on how to proceed. He kindly says I may contact him at any time to pick his brains. I promise I will be in touch again when I've made further progress and if I have any more questions. Now it's time to write the introduction to the book and knock the daily ramblings into a joined-up narrative. Quite a task. On top of that I set myself two targets: I will try to write a thousand words a day, and aim to finish the first draft of the opus by the end of October.

24th August

Matchless Matcham

This week *The Mousetrap* should have been playing the Buxton Opera House, claimed by many – and I'm among them – to be the architect Frank Matcham's masterpiece. I've been lucky to have played this theatre on a few occasions in opera and musicals, but never in a play. And now it's not happening.

Last year's tour took in several of Matcham's theatres, including Bristol's Hippodrome, Blackpool's Grand, The Devonshire Park, Eastbourne, Theatre Royal, Nottingham, and one which was new to me, The King's in Southsea. I spent a fascinating afternoon with the archivist there having a guided tour, and I'm now the owner of two paintings by former artists in residence, giving their perspective of the building's distinctive façade. The pictures have pride of place at the top of my stairs and in the sitting room. A daily reminder of Matcham's gift, and the fact that I was an actor until seven months ago.

Over the years I've performed in many of his theatres. Sometimes there was the added bonus of a long engagement: in pantomime (*Sleeping Beauty*) at Theatre Royal, Wakefield; a rep season at Cheltenham's Everyman; and a two-year stint in *Sound of Music* at the London Palladium.

Millions will have been dazzled by his brilliance when *Strictly* pays its annual pilgrimage to The Tower Ballroom. Another one of his. At one time there was hardly a major town or city that didn't boast a theatre by this doyen of architects. Now, only two dozen survive. I'm lucky to have one close by in Richmond.

The man was a genius. You immediately feel at home in a house that Frank built.

27th August

The Seasons Alter

Although it's still officially British Summer Time, thoughts start to turn to preparations for winter. It pays to plan ahead. Today I have my central heating boiler serviced. The family firm I use are very reliable and reasonable. The young son of the outfit, who confusingly shares the same Christian name as his father, assures me that they will always come out in an emergency, even on Christmas Eve. Now that's what I call Five Star Service.

And there are outdoor jobs, too. Soon it will be time for the clearing of leaves; planting bulbs; putting the garden to sleep for winter; and dreaming of a better spring next year, full of flowers but pandemic-free. Please God.

28th August

Voice Workout

There's a bit of a false start this morning. My scheduled voice surgery with Marina has to be postponed until this afternoon as she has had travel issues. I look upon this as a mixed blessing in a way. It's true I have more energy in the morning but I now have plenty of time to warm up and longer to prepare.

The wait was worth it. Marina is a fine teacher, patient and encouraging. But she is no pushover. At several times during the hour-long virtual seminar she is frank in her criticism but it is always constructive.

When, towards the end of the session, she compliments me: "You take direction well," I respond: "Well, what's the point of paying for expert advice, if you ignore it?"

She promises to send me detailed notes on the selected pieces later today. Can't wait for the recording on 17th September in the studios of Crying Out Loud – a perfect name for a voice agency. Before then, daily practice will be required.

29th August

Progress Report

I post on Facebook today for the first time in a while. Some friends have been worried that ill health or boredom might be the reason for my silence. I confirm that it's because of the book. Editing the posts of the last five months is laborious and leaves no scope for daily musings. The timing is deliberate: 7,000 words were reached yesterday.

My target is challenging: 1,000 words a day. And I want to reach *The End* by the end of October. That's a lot of words. But I've always had a lot to say for myself. As my English teacher, Mr Robbins, took delight in saying: "Francis fancies his chances!"

He was nicknamed Crow because of his prominent beak, and his black, flapping, long-sleeved academic gown. He had a sharp tongue, certainly, but his love for literature, and the works of Shakespeare in particular, were infectious. I caught the bug from him and retrospectively am deeply grateful.

As another month closes I look forward to the fresh opportunities the future holds. I'm relearning my solo piece *Chapel, Chums and Chips: a Boy's-Eye View of Swansea Folk*, with the aim of taking it on the road again next year. In the meantime I'm going to share its thirteen chapters every Saturday from October 3rd, until the year's end, 'Live at Five' on Facebook.

Ambitious, but I'm only proving what the wise old Crow said was true.

SEVEN

SEPTEMBER SONG

"And all at once summer collapsed into fall."
(Oscar Wilde)

2nd September

The Kew Quartet
And now we are four; not our usual two. Jane – Dewey, not Harvey – and I have been enjoying breakfast walks in Kew most Wednesdays since its gates were reopened after lockdown. This morning we are joined by our friends David and Margarette Harmer who have driven up from St John's – an enchanting Surrey village on the outskirts of Woking. I have stayed with them in their cosy cottage twice over the last dozen years when first *Chitty Chitty Bang Bang* and then *The Mousetrap* played the New Victoria. The Harmers are great hosts and are jolly good company.

Both of them have been very encouraging in their responses to my Facebook diary and are equally keen to learn how the book is coming along. David is a talented artist and has been very busy during this Corona year. And his paintings have been selling well of late.

A seed is sown in the gardens…

Perhaps David might consider illustrating 'The Write Escape'? We'll see.

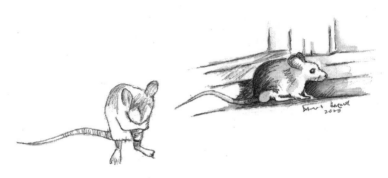

Mouse looking for an escape

6th September

Blasted Vegetarians

As I've previously mentioned, I love my friends David Roughan and Kelly Meadows dearly, but they are vegetarians, and I find this hard to forgive. I am joking, of course. But it is an effort not to serve up the same old recipe each time. This being said, I know there are favourites this couple never tire of having.

This is a working supper. They are here to assemble my extending tripod, which arrived on my doorstep earlier in the week. A generous gift from them. Once the telescopic legs are secure, and the phone clamped in place, we try some dry runs in readiness for my first Live at Five on Facebook, screening on 3rd October. We film in portrait not landscape and my little Samsung Galaxy 10 rises to the occasion and produces good picture quality, once my two directors have got the lighting right. They are both experienced teachers, and I find their instructions clear and simple. However, I do take notes as I find it hard to remember technical procedures. I'm out of my depth. Learning lines is a different matter.

Sensing my unease, Kelly and David promise that they will be in attendance on 3rd October to make sure there are no hitches, and to lend moral support.

Such care and kindness deserves its reward, so I give them a three-course meal.

1. Mushroom Soup.
2. Beetroot and feta tray bake, with hazelnuts and rocket, and drizzled with orange dressing.
3. Pannacotta with fresh raspberries and coulis.

I will pass on the recipe for the starter as it's a soup I've been making for almost twenty years. The recipe for the main course can be found on the Waitrose website. I used ready-made puff pastry, but the dish does feature my own beetroot and rocket, both grown from seed. The dessert is shop-bought but I do make an effort and use half the raspberries to make a coulis.

But the soup is all my own work, though the recipe is not. It was given to me by Veronica Willoughby after she served it as part of a splendid Sunday lunch in Little Missenden in the early Noughties. I include it here.

Veronica's Cream of Mushroom Soup

Ingredients

- 8oz/225g mushrooms
- 1 small onion
- 15 fluid oz/425ml chicken stock (not today, I use vegetable stock for K§D)
- 10 fluid oz/275ml milk
- 2oz/50g butter
- 1 dessertspoon of soy sauce
- salt and pepper to taste
- 1oz/25g plain flour

Method

- Melt half the butter in a saucepan over a moderate heat. Add the chopped onion and cook gently until golden brown. Chop the mushrooms, including stalks, and put into the pan. Stir briefly so they absorb some of the buttery juices before pouring in the stock. Cover and simmer for 15 minutes. In a separate small saucepan melt the remaining butter over low heat and stir in the flour and beat briskly with a wooden spoon to make a roux, with no lumps. Put the roux into a liquidiser with the soup, milk and soy sauce. Blend on full power until the mixture is smooth, about 30 seconds.
- At this stage the soup can be stored overnight in the fridge. Reheat over a gentle heat, constantly stirring so the soup doesn't catch and to prevent lumps forming. If they do, whirl in the liquidiser for a few seconds.
- I can guarantee you'll never taste finer in any other diner!

9th September

Blessed Carnivores

There are no fears of getting a vegetarian meal when I make my way to Holly's in Mortlake, three days later. That would be anathema to my fellow carnivore. When I arrive I spot mint sauce on the already-laid table and catch the unmistakable smell of lamb roasting. But this treat is on hold until Holly has put me through my paces: a speed-run of *Chapel, Chums and Chips* in readiness for my weekly Live at Five Saturday sessions on Facebook. I think the storytelling will be more effective if I can speak from memory directly to the camera and not have my head buried in a script. Holly, copy in hand, listens attentively, corrects me when I go wrong and prompts me when I dry. She also gives some brilliant notes. I take them on board as she is an experienced director, and I respect her judgment and taste.

Having heard my 'dicky birds' she dons her apron and makes the gravy. All I have to do is pour us each a glass of wine, carve the joint, and tuck in and eat.

Long live lamb! It didn't die in vain.

10th September

The Green Gardener

I hit a snag today. The plan was to harvest the green tomatoes ready to make Chapel Chutney, my treasured, much-used recipe from Vera Batty. When the small hard fruits are washed, I weigh them. Disappointingly, they tip the scales at 12oz. I cross the road to David in Number 18 to scrounge enough to make up a pound. A cheek, I know, but as I gave him the plants way back in April, I don't feel too guilty. He hands over half a dozen tomatoes willingly. In return I promise that he and Mary will be rewarded with a jar of the golden elixir tomorrow when the sugar, vinegar and spices have worked their alchemy on the apples, onions and the precious green jewels.

Back in number 23 I get to work in the kitchen. I prepare to weep once more over the onions. I soak them in cold water for half an hour as I find this makes them easier to peel and not as eye-watering. There is a good hour of chopping, processing and stirring ahead until the mixture reaches a jam-like consistency. The cooking process takes about forty minutes. Turmeric comes to the party first, followed five minutes later by ground cloves, cayenne and ginger. After a further ten minutes, I turn off the heat and add the final spice: a generous handful of mustard seeds. Cover with a damp tea towel and leave to stand overnight. Then it will be ready for bottling and sampling. That's the best part and reward for the months of anticipation, and the attention the plants have received.

I make a note that next year I will sow seeds of a larger variety of tomato and hope for a better yield. Back in March I had to accept whatever was on offer as demand was high and seeds were scarce.

Another time I won't be so *green*.

13th September

The Ides of September. Time to Wind Up?

Now seems as good a time as any to draw my ramblings to a close. Seven months have passed since "the Ides of March", when we all experienced the abrupt end to life as we had known it pre-pandemic. *The Mousetrap* seems a distant memory to me. It feels as if it happened to a different person. I suppose we all have been affected and are "changed utterly".

Alarmingly, the number of new cases of Covid-19 is rising by the day, as are the deaths. The optimism of early July has been replaced by September's stark reality that we're not shot of the virus yet, not by any means. The unemployment figures are rising as is anxiety over the way forward. One thing is certain: the repercussions will be felt for decades to come. The cost to the nation's health, prosperity and well-being is incalculable. Our national debt is no longer measured in billions but in trillions. Payback will be long and hard. A punishing legacy for the younger generation. The road will be muddy and rough, but I truly believe, along with the songwriter, that we will get there. God only knows how, but we will.

When the pandemic took away my livelihood, and the great love of my life, performing, I felt there was a huge creative void that needed to be filled. I sought – and have found – my escape in writing, hence the title of this tome. The circumstances that engendered this change of direction were catastrophic and lamentable, of course, and I wish they hadn't occurred; but out of despair sprang the joy of a new beginning. Obviously, the challenge of writing a thousand words a day has been a good discipline; but also of inestimable value for my self-esteem and mental health. And I have been buoyed by the responses I have received from friends, many of them new. Indeed, I would never have embarked on this exercise if it hadn't been for the encouragement of several kindly souls chorusing: "John, you must put these posts into a book."

Looking back over the last seven months, there are reasons to be cheerful. I have gained new friends; got to know more of my neighbours; sadly lost one agent, lovely Lisa, but gladly found a replacement in Simon, a human dynamo; made a voice demo; relearned *Chapel, Chums and Chips*; and been taught how to self-video – so important when face-to-face interviews and meetings will be strictly limited while there is still the risk of catching Covid. Open auditions won't be happening anytime soon.

I feel better equipped now to face the struggles that undoubtedly lie ahead; and as I reach the end of these musings, the seasons have come full circle. British Summer Time will soon be ending. The garden has been put to sleep, the bulbs are snug in their beds and the leaves will soon be cleared. We look forward to a better spring.

If you've read this far it means two things: I've engaged your interest, and I'm in print. I've loved sharing my thoughts with you.

In the not-too-distant future I hope you might, once more, hear me "shouting in the evening." That's what Michael Gambon calls acting. (And, *Clang!* – yes, I have worked with him.) And it's not just plays I pine for: I want to sing in opera again, and in another West End musical while the lungs are

Corona-free and I'm still good on my legs. *Arlene, get that '10' paddle ready!*

Time to put down this pen now and explore new avenues, but I will continue to read and write, and hope!

For now, this 'tail' is told.

P.S. Am I a man or a mouse? Dear reader, you decide.

RECIPE INDEX

WITH THANKS...

The author is grateful to the following for giving permission to reproduce their poems; namely:

Shauna Darling Robertson for 'Dancing with Life' from *Saturdays at the Imaginarium* (Troika 2020)

Alison Skelton for 'The Watergate of Castle Urquhart'

Tony Aldridge for 'The Glove'

And to David Higham Associates, literary agents, and to the copyright holder, The Dylan Thomas Trust, for permission to quote from *Under Milk Wood: The Definitive Edition* (Published by Weidenfeld & Nicolson)

16-10-15

11932778

197241